What Readers, Writing Circle Members, and Workshop Participants are saying about *FEAR OF WRITING*

"I really am thrilled with this new way of writing! It seems to bypass the clinical/critical mind and get straight to the creativity." Sandy Shairer, Tijeras, New Mexico

"Wow, I was laughing out loud at some of your skeleton plots! This is great stuff! I think our readers are really going to enjoy this contest." Krista Barrett, editor, The Writer Gazette, www.writergazette.com

"I'm excited to have won the contest (my first!), and even more thrilled to be the recipient of your book. I look forward to reading it and growing as a writer as I use more of your exercises." Dena Harris, Madison, North Carolina, www.writergazette.com/contestfear.shtml

"It screams SAFE!" Sallye Beranak, Ft. Collins, Colorado

"I'd been battling a case of writer's block ever since the terrorist attack on Sept. 11. Each word needed to be squeezed out of me like lemon juice, and when it hit the page it was just as sour. And then I read *Jack's House*. Every obstacle Helen encountered, every fear, every thought she had, paralleled my own troubles so completely I was stunned. I'd been terrified that my fiction was trivial, meaningless, and without purpose, but when I finished reading *Jack's House* I understood what I needed to do. This was the miracle I'd been searching for." Jenny Turner, Stevens Pt., Wisconsin,

"Thank you! Your [book excerpt] has given me two gifts—the

knowledge that others are fighting the same inner battle of writing insecurity and, more importantly, that we can laugh at these insecurities and write anyway!" Reader feedback, *Innerself*, www.innerself.com/Miscellaneous/comments/fear _writing_Comments.htm

"It really got them going. Even one student who never liked to write and usually stalled around was engaged." Micah Roseberry, teacher and principal, Country Day School, Taos, New Mexico, on using the Fertile Material exercises with her sixth graders

"I found a big piece of myself as I read this [book excerpt]. I thank the author for her courage in writing about her fear of writing in such a provoking manner." More reader feedback, Innerself.com book excerpt

"Howdy, I'd like to request [an online invoice] for your book. Even at 6:30 a.m., sans my first cup of coffee, the Chapter One excerpt made me laugh, it was so on target. I've got to read on so I can find out what's going to happen to me!" via email, Sally McKissack-Lauck, Baton Rouge, Louisiana

"Lately I've been learning about going into feelings rather than avoiding them, but this is the first time I've been introduced to the idea of going straight into the fear of writing. What a wonderful, beautiful twist for me to see." More reader feedback, Innerself.com book excerpt

"Milli's Fertile Material exercises have helped me go from a closet writer who dreamed of writing a novel when I retire, to a writer who began writing a book during what for me is the annual time crunch—tax season!" Skip Pedlar, CPA, Taos, New Mexico

"SO, WHAT *IS* FERTILE MATERIAL?"

This book contains 112 "Fertile Material" writing exercises (see index for exercise titles). Thornton invented the Fertile Material after she failed to find writing books featuring the type of exercises she craved. She longed for exercises that would be fun to use—rather than academic, introspective, or list-oriented. Milli wanted writing exercises to cause her to write stories: complete with characters, dialogue and action. It has since been demonstrated, in many workshops and writing circle sessions, that anyone can use the Fertile Material to launch into story writing. It works instantly; no previous experience required. Commitment-wise, too, the Fertile Material works well at any level; including thumbnails and story fragments. As one reader put it:

"One great thing about the Fertile Material is that I can take a break from a longer piece (such as my novel #2) and have some real fun! But the best part about the exercises is that each story can be saved and worked on again later—either as a novel or as a story that might be worth submitting to a magazine or writing contest." Jennifer Turner, Stevens Pt., Wisconsin

The sequel, *Son of Fear of Writing*, is slated for release in 2004. *Son of* (and subsequent sequels) will publish pieces created by people from all walks of life who have written stories and vignettes using the exercises in this book. The sequel introduces a fresh batch of Fertile Material—along with workshop tools such as "Name Soup" and "Swear Like an Aussie." Milli's habit is to do the Fertile Material alongside her workshop and writing circle groups, and she plans to produce an e-book of her own Fertile Material stories. Watch for these releases at fearofwriting.com.

FEAR OF
WRITING

FEAR OF WRITING

Milli Thornton

www.fearofwriting.com

Word Nerd Press
P.O. Box 200
Ranchos de Taos, NM 87557 USA
Enquiries: booksales@fearofwriting.com

Library of Congress Number: 99-91689
ISBN (Imprint Books edition):   1-59109-818-1

Printed in the United States of America. Cover and book design by Milli
Thornton. Cover title "Bloody" font created by Jim Fordyce © 1994.

To purchase additional copies of this book:
www.fearofwriting.com or
USA toll-free 1-866-308-6235

For Brian & Bonnie, with love
For Caster & Camille, with a meow
For Jen, with warm thanks for the inspiration,
the laughter and the camaraderie

ACKNOWLEDGMENTS

HEARTFELT THANKS to the kind people who have helped me raise *Fear of Writing* from an embryo to a teenager: Ranchos Coffee Co., Taos, New Mexico, for the coffeehouse vibes during my Friday writing sessions and to Geri and Lenore for providing my first book signing space; Steve Andrus, for capturing the *Fear of Writing* doggie in all his arsonist glory; my husband, Brian Williams, for designing the bumper sticker and for launching a website I am proud of; Skip Pedlar and Leigh Lauck, for helping me test drive the Fertile Material exercises; Adrien Gordon of Gordon & Riggs, for triggering my first reviews; Sandy Misage, owner and host at the Hydration Café, Santa Fe, for providing my first workshop space; Jennifer Turner, for her book review at the Peacock Chronicle; Cindy Robison, for her graphic design work on the *Fear of Writing* T-shirts, coffee mugs, and mouse pads; and, last but not least—JEN, for setting it all off with an innocent remark!

CONTENTS

5. FERTILE MATERIAL UNLIMITED

GETTING MILK FROM THE COCONUT

SUFFERING COMES WITH THE TURF

Is writing supposed to be fun?

Surely, it's better to suffer. It will make our writing real—give it depth and integrity.

If we're not going to suffer, we should at least work hard. We should be disciplined. We should think in terms of productivity. A writer's not going to have a career to speak of unless she's producing at least 1,000 words per day, right? If you get right down to it, it's really a number crunching game. Or so the rumor goes.

Every writer has a personal tale about the hardships of writing. And we all know that writing is a lonely business. Martin Myers made this kind of alienation adorably quotable when he said: "First you're an unknown, then you write one book and you move up to obscurity."

But this swallowing gulf is no laughing matter. As we chart our descent into the nether world of writing, honk if you know the story already.

Outside, the sun is shining and the robins are happily pulling up worms. Inside your snug little home, you're staring into the abyss. The terror of facing that empty page is only surpassed by the numbness of your decomposing mind.

Just moments ago you were a lively specimen of resourceful humanity. Moments ago you were finding ways to speed through your chores and commitments in order to allow yourself some precious writing time. But, now that you're seated in front of your favorite writing implements, you uncover the bleak truth. You have nothing to say. You are less inspired than the lowliest drone sorting microchips on the assembly line. You are empty. Soulless. Mere space dust inhabiting a warm body. You have no right to aspire to that auspicious title: Writer. Where did you come up with the nerve to even think it?

OK, so you've managed to convince your primal brain stem these negative messages are melodramatic. You are *not* empty. You are not a zombie from the twilight zone. While waiting in line at the drive-up bank, you even had "an idea" and now you intend to write it down. You're no lightweight.

In fact, you have some guts and you plan to use them. How can you not be a writer? It's in your blood. It permeates every atom of your mortal being. It reaches all the way to your higher self. Even your past lives were spent as royal scribes in Egypt or poets in Atlantis.

Triumphantly, you break those chains of oppression. You commit some tentative words to paper. One line follows another and "Voila!" you have a paragraph.

You resist the urge to reread what you've managed to get down. You forge ahead: One paragraph becomes two, and then three, and then five. If the dog doesn't throw up again or the phone doesn't ring, you may even write two pages today. You are doing it! You're writing. You have defied the laws of emptiness. You are a god of creation.

But, the internal drag is taking its toll. Even as you defeat inertia to get those valiant words down on paper or typed onto the screen, you are faced with another self-evident truth: You are boring. Your writing would put insomniacs to sleep. You've seen livelier writing on the label peeling from the dank bottle of dishwashing liquid under your kitchen sink.

Yesterday you finished reading a mind-blowing novel by a twenty-three-year-old Asian author. He learned English only six months prior to writing his book. He wrote the entire book in Oriental calligraphy, using a brush and ink inherited from his great-great-grandfather, and then transcribed it into grammatically perfect English for his publisher in New York.

His prose is fluid, scintillating—nearly translucent in its candidness and lack of clutter. It's his first book, and yet he writes with the sensitivity and depth of a literary giant. His ancestors spring to life within the pages of his book; they say some of the funniest, wisest, most memorable things you've ever encountered. The writerly portrayal of this intricate, exotic foreign culture renders you speechless with admiration.

The book has won awards and has found a permanent niche on the bestseller's list. The author is under contract for three more novels. He writes blurbs for the covers of other people's books, and his name is sheer unadulterated gold in the publishing industry. Everyone wants a talisman; everyone wants a piece of his literary magic.

Meanwhile, sunk in a private morass of shame and self-loathing, you sit in front of the mundane passage you've written. You reread your words and reel in shock. It's blindingly obvious that you should give up now to save your family from the pain of watching you bomb out. Your paltry effort should be fed to the pigs for breakfast—with salt and pepper and plenty of ketchup. At least make it palatable for the pigs!

The rush of inspiration you felt in line at the bank is now in ashes on the page. You're embarrassed that you ever bragged to your friends about being a writer. Bragging leaves you no room to exit gracefully. Bragging leaves you no pride and no way to resume a normal life. If you give up now, your friends will know what a weakling you are and they'll never let you live it down.

Why would anyone want to suffer this way? You sit there, dripping with failure; pungent with the sweat of your fruitless labor. You remember that you go through this same horror scene every time you try to write. You always start on an innocent high, but then you degenerate into writing hell.

By the time the hounds of hell regurgitate you, you're limp with defeat. Your skin crawls with self-revulsion. Looking up from your mundane passage, you observe the ordinary world: You can't help but notice that your family and friends aren't being auto-consumed by this tapeworm called writing. You long to veg out in front of the TV with the kind of serenity you see others reveling in as their birthright.

You look in the mirror and tell yourself to "get a life." You decide to exercise at the gym whenever the urge to write strikes. You can put your nervous energy to good use at the gym instead of doing all that unhealthy introspection. Instead of agonizing like a word miser over what you have or haven't written.

The concept "writing is fun" is ludicrous. Experience has proven it beyond a shred of doubt. Fun for others, maybe, but never for you.

Still, you are curious to see which panacea will be on offer here. You remind yourself, since you've given up writing to lead a healthy lifestyle, that you've got nothing to lose. You have no personal stake in it now. . . . Miraculously, this has killed off the hellhounds and smashed the mental blocks. You are now free to try the exercises in this book without expectation or attachment to outcome. You're a perfect Buddha ready to give into non-judgmental acceptance.

Well, if not a Buddha then a glutton for punishment. You've made up your mind to try these dang exercises just to prove what you already know: Writing is a torture chamber invented specifically with you in mind.

BEYOND THE PURGE

It pays to be in the right company. I'm personally acquainted with the hellhounds in Chapter One, so you're safe identifying with this story. I wasn't born having fun as a writer any more than you were. Nor did I believe, until recently, that fun was possible. I followed the compulsion to write because I had to; because, even buried in apathy or depression, the compulsion wouldn't go away.

I considered myself a failed writer and even a "fraud." I'd go through long seasons of not writing a thing. Which—as you may know yourself—is a death unlike any other.

What caused the painful dry spells where I would turn away from my creative expression? It was the heart malady called fear of writing. Medical doctors have yet to diagnose it; it's not even on the list.

The disease may be endemic everywhere, but we don't have the statistics to prove it. People are out there languishing in writing limbo. They're busy self-medicating in writers' chat rooms or with the latest writing book. Experiencing periods of remission and then sliding into paralysis again.

Many people with this affliction lead outwardly active lives. They might be writing books. They might even be published authors. Others are out there in the self-help mediums, such as workshops and writing groups, doing their physical therapy—reading their work out loud in the weekly meetings or standing up to declare: "I am an addict." Writing is still frightening, but they are finding ways to cope. Discussing the symptoms with others who understand the disease intimately can be therapeutic beyond measure.

The question begs to be asked: "Is there a cure for fear of writing?" Am I here to tell you I've discovered the antidote?

"Quick," you say, "spit it out! I believe in faith healing! Heal me with your words!"

I'm here to tell you there's no cure for fear of writing—except to feel it and use it in your work. The fear is part of the process; part of what deepens your cognition. The fear itself is not the poison. The poison is the paralysis which results from trying to isolate or purge it. You cannot purge it like a cancerous cell unless you're prepared to lose some part of yourself. Purging your fear is never a lasting cure: It belongs to you.

When your fear is acknowledged as an integral part of you it becomes transformative: a circulation of energy lending character to your work and giving you the strength to accept yourself. You could call it writing chi.

If you decide to accept your fear, this book will offer support. You'll encounter stories about fictional people who have the selfsame fear of writing, and the stories will give you hope. But there's nothing I can tell you that will do as much as your own process of accepting the fear. This book will give you a kick-start, through stories and exercises, and you will do the rest. You could call it writing self-empowerment.

As you empower your fear, you'll see the myths drop away. Haven't we always been told if we "buy into" fear dire things will happen? We'll become negative people. Others will shun us. The negativity will draw bad luck, or even accidents.

The old wives' tales originate from a simple, but profound, misunderstanding of fear. When the channel of what could be *evolutionary* fear is shut down, our lives cramp; our potential has limited energy to work with. Look around you for a day and observe this happening. Examples abound, both within and without.

Fear itself is blamed for this crippling effect—rather than the continual reflex of shutting down the flow of energy.

Fear has a bad name, and we've been taught to control it or expunge it from our lives. We can carry on the tradition and shoot the messenger or we can allow the fear to help us widen our boundaries.

Learning to allow your fear to participate is liberating. You'll find beauty inside which you didn't realize was there. You'll grow to like yourself more. Others will notice and want you around. Uncramping will bring you adventures. And— maybe best of all—you'll take off as a writer.

The exercises in this book will give you the material to start you on your journey. Chances are, you're already on this journey; you're simply out looking for some extra tools. Remember: The primary tool is yourself and your own capacity for growth. And you can go at your own speed. This healing is uniquely yours.

If you *wish* you could go on an adventure like the one I'm describing but see yourself as a timid person, you'll find baby steps here that anyone can try.

If you are already a vigorous writer—one who doesn't lose sleep over writer's block or dry spells—the exercises will help you unleash your imagination still further. As there is no limit to your imagination there is no way to wear it out. The more you flex it the more limber it becomes.

FERTILE MATERIAL: EXERCISES FOR WRITERDOM

Your imagination is like a dog kept indoors too long during rainy weather. If you let the dog out, what will it do? Probably roll in the mud, caper, bark for joy, shake its coat out, run fast with a stick in its mouth, and systematically sniff everything in the garden.

Humans look on in amusement when a dog plays. We think these are merely the simple pleasures of a dumb beast. But, let me tell you, that dog feels good inside. Humans feel superior—we think we're the "civilized" ones—but that dog is in touch with the universe.

Before you read the stories or try the exercises in this book, hold a ceremony for yourself. You don't have to burn sage in a miniature temple or invest in crystals and mandalas. Make it fancy, if you want to, but the crux of the ceremony should be a promise to yourself.

Promise to let out your imagination like a dog being let out to play. Promise not to suppress that dog. Even if you see the dog acting silly, don't try to cramp its style. That dog doesn't care what people think. Trust that doggie wisdom.

If you want to, give your dog a name. Write a passage about him—or her. Get to know your dog, because this dog is going to lead you on a journey for treasure.

Stop reading now so you can hold your ceremony.

* * *

Since we're here to embrace our fear, you may assume that the writing exercises in this book will all be searing, get-down-deep, soul-charting journeys. We could take that route. Learning about ourselves through serious introspection is a noble pursuit. . . . But, ultimately, it does not bring balance. Why? Because there's no true balance without fun.

Is writing supposed to be fun?

Yes!

The core of the book alternates between exercises and stories. While reading the stories, relax, enjoy. You'll absorb everything you need by getting involved with the characters' feelings. The stories are in the "Passive Zone." In the Passive Zone, you are receiving input and being entertained.

The writing exercises—dubbed "Fertile Material"—are in the "Active Zone." They are studded between the stories to provide a contrast in pace. Three exercises appear at the end of each of the four stories. But the first block of three will be in your face at the end of the next chapter. By then, you'll be prepared and you'll know how to use them. Have you ever made mashed potatoes from a box? Using the Fertile Material is as simple as making instant mashed potatoes.

The tally is 112 exercises—enough to keep you writing for months, even years, depending on what level you choose to go to with each exercise. Most of the Fertile Material can be found in the back of the book, beginning on page 191, in the section entitled "Fertile Material Unlimited." Included are the exercises to have fun with, exercises for your serious writing moods, and the one-liners—"Fertile Material Skeletons."

You will derive more freshness and value from each exercise if you resist the temptation to pre-read the Fertile Material section as just another slab of text. Try not to read an exercise until you're ready to use it. It may seem more comforting to read every last word in the book before you ever pick up your pen (you know what I mean . . . to avoid trying the writing exercises until you feel "ready"), but it's a false comfort. To work with your fear of writing, you need to be active.

You might have heard your grandmother lament on how the younger generation will sit around the house letting good blood silt up. Those pesky young'uns never want to *do* anything. Too much "passive zone" (TV and computer games) makes kids sluggish. Well, it's the same with writing. Reading every single word in the book first is another way to let your blood silt up. In all likelihood, you'll finish the book with good intentions; yet, somehow, there's never enough time in your hectic life to get a handle on those good ol' writing exercises.

As I've spent years myself—good writing years, when youth was still on my side—prostrate with this same sediment of the blood, I know the traps. Which means I'm not going to let *you* off the hook. You won't have to go to the gym to get your blood moving because you've just found yourself a new aerobics instructor. And I'm tough.

To begin with, this is not a bedtime book. Just as you would never dream of exercising aerobically right before you go to sleep, this book should be strictly a daytime pursuit. If you're lying in bed when you finish reading the next chapter, you're not about to get out of bed to tackle that first writing exercise. You're going to put the book down and drift into a guilty snooze. In bed the next night, you'll read "An Audience of Your Own" and then fall asleep and dream about having an audience for your writing. But the eye in the tower is watching you, so don't read this book in bed.

Plan to read even the Passive Zones when you're alert. If you pick up the book to finish reading one of the four long stories, make sure you'll have some time left over at the end for the—ugh—writing. Don't lull yourself with the illusion that during your next vacation you'll have some spare time for the

Fertile Material. If you commute to work by bus or train, use that time to take the plunge. Look for any small chink in your routine. A mere sliver, even ten minutes per day, is enough to get you started.

David A. Fryxell, author of nearly 1,000 magazine and newspaper articles, knows that the secret to having the time to write is to use the time that you've got. Even those fleeting, elusive minutes.

In his book *How to Write Fast (While Writing Well)*, Fryxell tells an eye-opener about a canny French chancellor, D'Aguesseau. The chancellor noticed that his wife habitually arrived at the dinner table roughly ten minutes late and (yes!) realized he could use the ten minutes each evening to write. Ten minutes each night becomes 60.7 hours over the span of a year. During his cleverly employed sixty hours per annum— while waiting for his tardy spouse and numerous hot French dinners—D'Aguesseau wrote a three-volume book. It became a bestseller when released in 1668.

Uh-oh. Now you're intimidated by these paragons of output. But while you're busy wallowing in the humiliation of being a Homer Simpson, do the exercises.

You will hate to reach the end of the next chapter. The end of Chapter Next is your showdown. Three pre-packaged writing exercises staring you in the face. The fear, the fear, oh the cruel fear. So much less traumatic to skip past those nasty little exercises—maybe skip ahead and read one of the stories.

"I can come back later," you tell yourself innocently.

Stop! Your attitude of innocence is a blind façade. Beneath that façade lurks the monster, Procrastination. And we all know that monsters are the biggest scaredy-cats ever.

The end of Chapter Next is where you dig in and start to build your writing abs. Pick up your pen, step up to that first exercise, and write. No, don't read all three exercises so you can pick the one that sounds the easiest to coast through. We're here to pack muscle. Begin at Exercise One.

Help! Someone dropped you into a vat of bubbling, icky fear and all you can write is cave man or cave woman grunts. Good. Keep grunting. You'll get there. After a while, you'll progress to crude language. Soon, you'll begin to use verbs. Your stick figures with speak balloons will blossom into real characters. Your thumbnail sketch will uncoil like a snake, becoming a plot that you can coax and charm out of your imagination and into the light.

This leap into fully developed prose may not happen for you during the first exercise. If your muscles are flabby, they're not going to snap into shape after one aerobics class. But go ahead and be devastated by your perception of colossal failure. Then get up off the floor and do it again. Keep that blood moving.

Don't sprain a muscle on your first day by attempting more than one exercise. Whenever you use a Fertile Material exercise, pretend it's the one and only writing exercise on the planet. Milk it for all it's worth. Focus on it like it's the only thing you'll ever get to write.

At first, the familiar failure issues may be clamoring in your head, and you'll be convinced you don't have much to say. Focus on the exercise and just keep going. You'll discover many layers of imagination patiently waiting to unfold themselves into your awareness.

. . . Just like levels of fitness in that insufferable gym class. Release those endorphins! Get that lymph pumping. People who exercise have an increased sense of well being.

You can have that feeling too.

HOW TO REAP AN ABUNDANT CROP

Many of the Fertile Material exercises were designed to give you a new attitude. As in: "You sure have an attitude, mister!" This is healthy and should not be repressed.

Let your characters be opinionated. Even if you feel hypocrisy or personal taboo creeping in, let it rip. Don't pretty it up for your grandmother. Don't try to be "PC" (politically correct).

If you are worried that something unconventional or sassy you've written might put someone's nose out of joint, then don't show it to that person. These exercises are not for other people to sanction; they're for your own brave dash to freedom. This is about creative and emotional self-rescue not about pleasing others.

You can learn new truths about yourself from whatever comes up when you begin to write without restraint.

Emotional rescue doesn't have to be painful. It can be zany and irreverent. It can be soft and subtle. It can be about switching roles or sexes—writing from a point of view you'd never thought to consider before.

You can experiment with writing in the voice of an animal, a baby, a forest, an alien. A baked potato on a paper plate at a family reunion. That's the snazzy thing about this game: You can write from anyone's point of view (including that square of chocolate you're about to sneak).

The specific set of rules you are going to flaunt is the

set governed by the critical voice in your head. Who wants to be governed by a critical voice? Now, instead of kowtowing to that voice, you can jump on your pencil-conjured Harley and ride like the wind in your studs and black leather. You can soar beyond the limits of your normal code of behavior and get away with it. You're doing it the safe way: The risks are only on paper. No speeding tickets, angry parents, or threatened spouse.

Another rule you can violate is the one that says you have to write "literature" every time you take up your pencil. The Fertile Material may often strike a familiar chord. You'll recognize stuff from everyday life, usually served up with a twist. The wackier exercises will mock credibility; maybe even ruffle your literary pride.

Don't shy away from being wacky. You can be literary and sage later—once you've loosened up and learned to flow.

Fear itself does not feature in the Fertile Material cues as much as you might expect. This doesn't mean you're not "embracing your fear." This book is here to stimulate writing sessions that encourage you to write more—and to write more often. Fear will surface as a by-product of the act of writing. "Oh, goody," I hear you say. Better than cramps, right?

More good news: Accepting the fear will build your momentum. The emotional activity gets that sludgy blood flowing, which will bring you the healing. The stagnation of *paralyzed* fear will drop away. In a chain reaction, all your emotions will become more vibrant. E-motion. The word itself signals "motion"—the movement of "e"nergy.

Each Fertile Material exercise is like an encapsulated screenplay or novel: the raw material for constructing a story. At first this may seem too plotted for your comfort. The exercises were designed this way to help you cultivate the habit of being specific. Visualize the ability to be specific as another muscle in your repertoire. Exercise that muscle!

You don't have to produce a book or movie every time

you play with the Fertile Material. But developing these mini-plots will show you the gems your imagination is capable of. The first few gems may be diamonds in the rough, but trust the lapidary process and keep mining for those nuggets.

When you're pottering with the plots, don't spoil your fun by worrying about an ending for your story. Coming up with a clever ending can be a lot of pressure for any writer. At this stage in the game, our focus is on the magic of learning to flow. 112: Leave some of them with no endings. It's liberating.

If your story zigzags all over the rodeo, doesn't follow a chronological line or even stick to the facts, then you need to suspect you might be having fun. Let yourself be messy. Tell mother you'll clean your room later—preferably when you are older and stuffier and believe like mother does that neatness is next door to sainthood.

And don't confuse neatness with being specific. Being specific is delving into the sensory realms, drenching yourself in curiosity, and then reporting back to the surface world with what you've observed.

Pretend you are writing a report for someone who has been exposed to sensory deprivation for a week. It's your job to provide him with richness of input, so he will revive from numbness and learn to function normally again. The range of what you can report to help your patient reconnect with life runs the gamut: taste, texture, shape, aroma, sound, visuals, thoughts, feelings and dialogue.

Once you've acquired basic Fertile Material skills—the ability to backflip into a different point of view and use all five senses to be specific—you can take these skills anywhere and be sparked into inspiration. Even that ordinary bug crawling in the grass can signify a new world to explore. Write from the bug's point of view; find out how it feels about life.

Hey! First I rip away the rulebook, and then I give you a replacement package of rules to apply. Take it easy on yourself. For example, don't fret if you start by following the mini-plot as outlined in the exercise and then end up going off on a tangent. The most important thing is to tap into a flow. The goal is to express yourself.

But what if you can't think of anything to write? If you feel as if you can't for the life of you drum up a "story line," begin by describing your character. Mention name, age, eye color, job. It doesn't have to be realism. You can be as "out there" as you wanna be. A pink-haired mortician? You bet.

What town/city does Character X live in? If you're nervous about being authentic with a real town or city then make one up. When is Character X's birthday? Talk about a family member who really irritates X as well as one family member he really loves.

What is Character G's financial situation? What are her dreams and goals? Does she harbor a secret? Whom is she hiding her secret from?

What is Character M most satisfied and dissatisfied with in his life? What special talent was he born with? Does he use his talent or let it go to waste?

What are Character Q's favorite foods? (Hmm, does she have any food allergies?) What is 100% guaranteed to make Q angry? Amused? Motivated? Subdued?

Now: a Fertile Material scenario. The saga of an old lady and her dog making a last stand against developers. They want her to leave the home she has inhabited for fifty-seven years so they can bulldoze it and put up a shopping mall.

You can see this character in your mind, but you don't know where to start. You don't know how to build a meaningful tale from such scraps. You're afraid you'll write something that won't sound real or authentic. After all, this is a human epic of endurance, conflict, tragedy, and social decline. How could li'l ol' you possibly do it justice?

First off: Bring it back down from the clouds. Remember your ceremony? You are not here to produce literature; you're just letting your dog off its leash. Don't over-inflate the picture to something so grandiose it cripples your desire to write. This is a story about a stubborn old woman. Everyone can relate to that.

Secondly: Don't pressure yourself to sound perfect or even warmed up yet. All writers need to start somewhere. Experienced authors unleash themselves by writing messy raw stuff known as the first draft.

It's not going to destroy the kingdom if your opening sentences are unadorned. You may be tempted to label them "juvenile," but the basics are not juvenile—just basic. Every good recipe starts with basic, familiar ingredients.

Give your heroine a name. Describe her. Make a start.

> *Aggie Blintz is small with squinty eyes. Her slippers are shabby. She lives in Pasadena. She's dirt poor and relies on food stamps, but Aggie's pride is fierce. Not even eighty-seven years of poverty can tame her pride.*

Next, bring in the big, mean developer. Bring in some action and interplay between the antagonists. Don't be afraid to use dramatics and exaggeration. Don't be afraid to be black and white. Make that bad guy BAD.

> *Mr. Schmuck from Hartless Malls Inc. says she has to get out now. He says they have court orders to evict her. Aggie's watching a soap opera; she pretends not to hear him. Her Chihuahua, Caesar, is growling. While Aggie watches a Pepto-Bismol commercial with the volume maxed out, Caesar nips the intruder on the ankle. Schmuck's face turns bankrupt-red. He storms out of the shack, yelling, "I'll see you in court!"*

> *"Good boy!" Aggie smirks and pats*
> *Caesar on the head. She gives him a pork*
> *chop bone to reward his loyalty.*

This doesn't mean you have to write rudimentary fiction for the rest of your life. The trick here is to use simple, graphic details—and avoid the temptation of trying to produce something polished or "ready for publication."

Trying to write to high standards puts us on our best behavior and makes us sound stilted. We're trying to *lose* our inhibitions . . . like an adult playing Twister for the first time since childhood. What a relief to let go and behave like a nut for a while!

But magic is happening, too, as you tinker with your building blocks and recite your ABCs. If you write the basics for long enough—and, often, you'll need only a few sentences for this—you will spark a connection to your characters. Then all you have to do is follow the thread.

A few choice words and the reader is fuming over the diabolical Mr. Schmuck. And what about Caesar, that feisty Chihuahua? Aggie's tiny pet has big instincts re Schmuckipoo that cannot be denied. To begin with, you might decide to develop the story from the munchkin's point of view. Later, you might allow the baddy to tell the story from his standpoint. What outlandish things will Schmuck say in defense of himself and his fiendish lust for profit?

Don't worry if you suddenly change styles or voices in midstream. Just keep that blood moving.

A handy trick to jumpstart the flow is to keep a stock of names at your disposal. Look for names that sound exotic or comical. This trick will encourage your characters to wake up and start creating havoc—like Frankenstein coming to life and crashing through the lab with his ungainly monster walk, intent on his own desires.

Wouldn't you find it easier to be slapstick or inventive

with a character called Pierre Onion than one by the name of Pete Martin?

You could go to the bookstore and buy a painstakingly researched book of names designed for use by authors. Such a book will provide you with exhaustive lists of names and their meanings, derivatives, and backgrounds. This kind of authenticity is invaluable for historical romances or to lend symbolism to your detective's name (for that crime novel we all plan to write someday).

But don't cheat yourself of fun when it comes to using silly or extravagant names with the Fertile Material. That perfect, zany name from your private collection may be just what you need to flesh out a villain brewing in your mind or give a character a juicy personality twist.

Sources for amateur name hunting: the phone book (Mutz, Oddson, Clotworthy); *Roget's Super Thesaurus* (how about Mother Lode Wilson for a gold digger looking for a rich husband?); signs while traveling, including shingles (Dr. Pill). Keep a pocket notebook handy to jot down your discoveries.

An example of name play from the Fertile Material:

> ***SLEIGHT OF HAND*** *Your name's Yolanda Leadbelly and you are a handwriting analyst for a big company. You have your own office up in the personnel division. The company is pioneering the use of your skills for the hiring and firing of employees and management. So far, they have kept you busy analyzing handwriting samples from the current employee pool. Then, one day, a secret report comes across your desk: Disturbing trends are indicated in the crazy loops and heavy pressure used by the writer. You find out this report was written by Vidor DeBella, Mr. Executive Director himself. What is your next move?*

Many people associate handwriting analysis with an unconventional lifestyle. Our character, Yolanda Leadbelly, has an offbeat name in keeping with this image of the unorthodox. Chances are, Yolanda is viewed as something of a wildcat in the business environment simply because her vocation does not fit the mold.

While we've got this exercise in front of us, let's slip in another skill to help encourage a writing flow. Don't be afraid to repeat or rephrase details from the exercise to help you get started—as in high school, when the teacher expected you to parrot the assignment in the opening lines of your essay.

My name is Yolanda Leadbelly and I am a handwriting analyst for a large company. The company's name is LaSalle Industries. LaSalle was founded in 1896, and it was a traditional company for its first 101 years in business. But then a revolutionary thinker arrived and created scandal in the ranks. In 1997, LaSalle took on a progressive CEO with a spooky Transylvanian kind of name: Vidor DeBella. DeBella hacked at the old cobwebs and trucked in modernized policies.

The most unpopular change was the system of handwriting checks to evaluate all personnel. This insulted the loyal employees and threatened the dishonest ones. Some said it was nothing but superstitious bunk. Others muttered that DeBella's pet policy was surely the work of the devil.

On my first day with the company, someone scrawled hate graffiti in red pen on a Manila folder while I was out of my office. This scared me, but it also made me mad. I became determined to stick it out.

Like the sketch about LaSalle Industries using handwriting analysis, some of the Fertile Material will give you an area of expertise to mess around with. Don't let this bamboozle you. Don't waste time researching graphology before writing about Yolanda Leadbelly's sleuthing adventures.

Instead, use suggestion. Anyone is qualified to employ loaded imagery—in this case, imagery connected with handwriting such as crazy loops and heavy pressure—to keep the story humming along and achieve your aim of freewheeling expression. You don't have to be an expert on a subject to use suggestion in your writing.

Don't get me wrong: I'm not pooh-poohing library research or careful checking of facts. But, there's an appropriate place for it in your writing. If you stop writing in the middle of a free association exercise to bury yourself in reference books, you'll strangle the flow. Don't trap yourself in the linear world where everything runs on rules.

Stride in there boldly. Ad lib on that topic you're certain you know zip about. The results will give you more proof that your imagination is an adroit but under-exercised commodity. Let your imagination surprise you. In gratitude, your characters will get up and do the boogie-woogie on the page.

If you feel out of your depth with the plotted exercises and feel the need for something simple to get you started, use the Fertile Material Skeletons (page 208). The Skeletons are one-liners and can be used as baby steps if needed. But first try "Play Big" on page 23. It's not as scary as it looks.

After you plunge headfirst into the Fertile Material, you may soon feel as if you're wading in a bog of glutinous sludge. You'll be convinced everything you're writing is sheer "garbage." This is much more common than you dream it is. Keep going! Don't stop to read what you've written or lament over your dreary style. Lament while you write, but keep at it.

We've now arrived at the point where a smart editor would insist on a disclaimer, so allow me to disclaim.

I am not promising you'll feel like a million bucks or be having oodles of fun from the very first exercise. But if you persevere—work those basics—I do promise that, come what may, your imagination will crack open like a ripe coconut and you'll have the milk of plenty spilling all over the page.

Let yourself be a pagan at full moon writing with all that lunar magnetism. The linear world is for cubicle nerds. Even if you earn your living as a cubicle nerd, you can still write like a pagan. Forget those old English lessons and the pressures of "literature" for a while, and let yourself play.

FERTILE MATERIAL

PLAY BIG You are a musician in a sought-after jazz band. Your name is Clarence and you travel with the band for six months of every year, playing concert halls and jazz festivals. How old are you? Give the band a name. Choose your instrument. Portray the other band members and the feeling you get when you play together. Eleanor, a high fashion model, is interested in one of you. She has wiles and she uses them. Will the band survive her foxy tricks and secretive smile?

ONLY THE WISE You're a Siamese named Miniver* living in a genteel household of intellectuals. Your household is the epitome of elegance, fine breeding, and superlative taste. The only discordant note—at least, as far as *you* are concerned—is Zeus, that lower class mutt who rampages through the house causing havoc wherever he goes. You cannot understand how your beloved humans could suffer such an uncharacteristic lapse in good taste.

FORT RIVALRY One fine summer your dad builds you a tree house. It's on a vacant lot, so it is considered fair game. Neighborhood kids form a friendly gang and use secret passwords or coded knocks for admission to "the fort." There's a war going on; the gang's archenemy is a high school boy nicknamed "Praying Mantis." This would be the best summer of your life if it wasn't for that bossy redhead, Stuart McGill—the self-proclaimed five-star general of the fort. He thinks he runs the gang. Even adults do what Stewy McGill tells them to do!

---

*miniver *n.*, a white fur used for trimming garments, especially ceremonial robes, as of royalty

AN AUDIENCE OF YOUR OWN

Every writer desires his or her own audience. You may be shy about exposing your vulnerability to the world, but it's a perfectly natural impulse to yearn for readers to help celebrate your creations.

If you do feel ready to show your work to others, be kind to yourself and careful when choosing your readers. If you give your work to another writer (murmuring modestly, "Will you look at this for me if you have time?") there's every chance you will receive a critique in return.

H.G. Wells nailed it when he said: "No passion in the world is equal to the passion to alter someone else's draft."

If the critique you receive is crude—too sweeping, nit-picky, or negatively worded—it may be just the blow to your emerging self-esteem which can send you into regression.

If you feel you're not yet ready for critique, one way to avoid this situation is to be specific. First, contemplate what you hope to gain from sharing your work. If you merely want to share it with a reader, make that clear to the recipient of your manuscript. Go so far as to spell out that you do not wish to receive a critique on your work at this time.

It's quite another thing to purposely seek expert help for proofreading, grammar, manuscript formatting, or whatever you feel you need assistance with. There are people who can do it professionally while using sensitivity and objective encouragement. If you invite this kind of help, it can be a healthy and rewarding step on your writing path.

Remember: These are your creations. You have the power to choose who helps you—and whether you want help yet. You have the power to choose someone who will make it a positive experience for you.

Contrary to what college professors would have you believe, there's no such thing as a "higher authority" when it comes to your writing. Why? Because the essence of writing is *self*-expression. The professional side of writing which can be farmed out to experts—checking for repetition of a pet word, correcting punctuation quirks, etc.—is not the same thing as the primal act of self-expression.

There is only one you. And there's no proxy for your own unique voice.

On the brighter side of venturing into the world with your creations: A shot of positive reinforcement will do wonders for your desire to keep writing. If you have a friend who's into writing, try doing a Fertile Material exercise together and then read your stories to each other. Agree to forego critique. If you hunger to give each other feedback, stick to your feeling responses.

"I felt tears come to my eyes."

"That image you used reminds me of the time from my childhood when . . . "

"The funniest part of your story was when . . . "

"You've captured exactly how I feel!"

You will be pleasantly surprised at how much closure you can find in this way. Paradoxically, the simple act of hearing your partner's story will imbue you with acceptance for your own attempts. This may not be apparent the first time you write together. Give it a little time to kick in.

Some writers prefer more sizeable groups where they can read their work to a receptive audience. Should you decide to join a writers' group, go on your gut instincts. If you feel safe and supported, you're in the right place. If, instead of feeling supported you feel demoralized by cruel or uninvited critiquing, do yourself a kindness and find another group.

Most states in the USA have a professional support group for writers. Here in New Mexico it's SouthWest Writers (www.southwestwriters.org). SWW is a nonprofit educational organization, and among its functions is the critique group; one for all categories of writing. It also offers a professional critique service (for members) at a fair rate. Don't settle for a clumsy—even inaccurate—critique from fellow writers when you can get one from the pros. Do an Internet search for a group equivalent to SWW in your own area.

Other writers may harbor that famous compulsion to remodel your work and may even convince you it's "character building" to submit yourself to it. But, there are gentler ways to hone your expressions. Writing as often as you can make time for it is the most organic way to grow as a writer.

If you know you are not yet ready to face the world of critiques (no one says you ever have to be) and all you want is someone near and dear to share your sense of achievement, read your story out loud to the family pet. You are guaranteed to receive unselfish love and non-critical acceptance from this particular audience! And the act of reading your work aloud will be another liberation for you.

A special thrill comes with putting a manuscript into the mail—especially if you know someone at the other end is definitely going to read it. If you want to, you can send me a sample of your Fertile Material adventures, and I'll be your made-to-order audience. Your Fertile Material will also have a chance to appear in one of the sequels.

Guidelines for submission are on page 215.

Start your own Fertile Material writing circle:
www.fearofwriting.com/Writing-Circles.htm

ACCIDENTAL SALVATION

We stumble on it by accident.

It's mid-June, and my friend Jen and I are sitting in their home office where her husband, Phil, runs his livelihood by fax machine and phone. Phil's music career means they're often on the road for several months at a stretch.

Whenever Jen's in town, we snatch as much quality time as possible. We are laughing and talking in the office when Jen mentions a dream she had before we knew one another. She wants to share the dream with me. She digs out an old notebook and leafs to the appropriate page.

Knowing she honors me with her trust, I approach the notebook gently but with avid curiosity. Jen is a private person. She is shy and modest and will crawl into a shell if she doesn't feel safe. I leap at the chance for more insight into my friend's heart.

Dream – 14 Feb, 1997 – Sydney, Australia

An owl (brown with white specks) flies over and perches itself on a friend. She's very comfortable with it, and when she offers to hand it over to me I am nervous and hesitant. It comes over. It's so cute, but it keeps opening and closing its beak—and I'm not sure if the owl is feeling my fear and is afraid, too. It moves quickly and fans its feathers outward and then back toward its body, which agitates me. I'm trying to hand it back to my friend. She talks to it and says it wants to hang out with me. I'm relieved and surprised that we can understand each other. I tell it (it's a girl) that I'm more than happy to love it as long as it promises not to bite me, because I don't want to get rabies. I see that this owl has a long monkey's tail. I faintly remember a couple of us trying to look up information on her in a computer, because she's unusual. Then I'm at a fashion/Hollywood scene, and some people want to play and hang out with her. She has the essence of Laura, a 10-year-old girl I taught nine years ago, who was so cute, innocent and funny. I look inside this glass room and find that, while examining her, they have abused her in ignorance and her tail is bleeding at the base. I yell at them while I grab her and then take her out to try to heal her. She is like my little baby. Can't remember the rest.

I'm struck by the clarity of expression. The simple language is alive with sensitivity and emotional depth.

"You didn't tell me you're a writer!" I blurt when I get to the last line of the dream.

"I'm not," Jen says, with typical modesty. "It's just a dream I wrote down."

I refuse to buy her version of reality. The woman's a writer going to waste. I set about trying to encourage her to write, and I ask her if she'll write with me.

I am excited by the potential of what we might inspire in one another. After years of living as a "wounded" writer—wounded by invisible daggers of confidence loss—

I'm ready to heal and consolidate my connection to writing. I've been pouring out my writer's woes to Jen by letter and by phone (or face-to-face, whenever she's in town between Phil's tours) all the while ignorant of the exhilarating fact that I'm talking to another writer.

Now that I know I'm dealing with a closet writer, I don't let up with her. I tell her about the "writing practice" I've been fooling around with based on Natalie Goldberg's famous Zen method for curing writer's block. I suggest we try it together, and I'm delighted—and surprised—when Jen agrees to my plan.

Our inaugural session takes place at a local café and involves rituals of coffee and chocolate—the primal bonds I share with Jen—along with the intimacy of divulging our fears and insecurities. We sip espresso that first time and talk about our nerves. We are putting off opening our notebooks until we can avoid it no longer. We're both terrified we have "nothing to write about."

At first, our writing practice is self-conscious and full of the fear of failure. We brood on paper about our embarrassing hang-ups and the profound dread of expression. Jen dubs it "practice writing," because we feel like such amateurs.

A typical passage from one of my early notebooks:

> *I have a phobia about being shallow. When I read a novelist like Jane Hamilton, I visualize my own writing and am dismayed at how shallow and one-dimensional it seems. When will I ever be able to write like that? Multi-layered, with that brilliant plotting; a style that makes you feel you are privy to the inner life of a real person. A character in a book with greater depth than I have myself!*

Jen's old Sydney, Australia notebook is her own shy and scary platform for bemoaning and self-reproach:

> *My breathing is stifled as I subconsciously aim to control any expression of emotions. To be more alive is scarier than to seem half dead. If I didn't have so much garbage to hide, would the mirror of my mind remain strong and whole regardless of the amount of caffeine I might consume? Perhaps I need to remove and surrender the shame in order to allow my senses to buzz and flower with colors and fragrances. . . . I've always been fearful of strong sensations, though I know that most of my life I've been a walking volcano . . . full of fire and turmoil, building up pressure, periodically exploding and shifting—releasing the submerged life force. . . . Releasing my authentic self. . . .*

Jen and I meet for practice writing sessions as often as we can. We know that we have less than three weeks together before she has to leave town for another long tour. Over the course of eighteen days, our belief in this tentative freedom grows. We gain acceptance for our trembling attempts to get airborne by swapping notebooks at the end of each session. I read hers and she reads mine.

Gradually, our focus changes. We both still write the occasional passage about how incompetent we feel, but now we're also dabbling in characterization. Jen's first fictional sketch comes out of nowhere:

> *Her nails are rough and chipped, remnants of old sparkly purple nail polish raggedly*

spotting the tips of her fingers. Her cuticles are raw and oozing blood and clear fluid. She can't stop tapping her fingers nervously on the table. She reaches again for a cigarette but stops midway as she remembers the "No Smoking" sign. She grabs the heart-shaped locket hanging from her Italian gold link chain. It's already warm from being fondled for the last twenty minutes. Her eyes dart to her sides, searching for the face of the physician. She sighs, wondering how long she must endure this torture; wondering if her boyfriend is still breathing and whether life will ever be the same. She feels pissed off with him. She just can't help it. She nagged him over and over to wear his helmet when he went riding on his Harley (a pride and joy which she usually feels second place to). He would argue that a helmet—especially being legally forced to wear one—spoils the whole idea and reason for cruising. He enjoys the wind flapping his ears, the smell of the gravel and bitumen, the sound of the motor as it hits speeds over 65. Wearing a helmet is like riding in an enclosed vehicle—might as well be driving a VW. "But," she would desperately point out, "what about Gary Busey?" She remembers how she felt almost a guilty sense of relief when the local news announced the actor's motorcycle accident. Famous as an outspoken proponent of helmet-free motorcycle riding, Busey was severely injured in an accident; he suffered head injuries and was in a comatose state for nearly a week. She had hoped this near-

fatal example would finally sober her boy-
friend into reconsidering his view on wear-
ing helmets.

Knowing that her reality is far from languishing in waiting
rooms, chain-smoking and agonizing over motorcycle accident victims, I'm again struck by Jen's natural capacity for
creativity, imagination, and sensitivity. She continues to
insist she's not a writer, but I see beyond her protestations.
She's a textbook example of fear of writing, is all. Like me.

I show Jen my own fling at characterization. As a
procrastination measure before we opened our notebooks,
we'd been people-watching while sipping lattés at the out-
door café in Taos called Peak Espresso. My sketch is based
on a stranger who had passed our table but with a pinch of
invention thrown in:

Gus is 79 and wears red tennis shoes and a
baseball cap. He strides with a stoop and
has a pot belly. The sacks under his eyes
sag in warty layers. His full lips work like a
horse snatching barley from your hand and
he continually looks as if he's on the point of
saying something, but he can't seem to spit
it out. Whenever you talk with him, watery
eyes travel your face restlessly. As you re-
late an anecdote, he fires off his questions:
"How old is she?" "Where did she get the bi-
cycle?" "Which day did it happen?" "Where
does she work?" "Where does she live?" Gus
never responds with a statement beginning
with "I feel . . . " He makes some pronounce-
ment about the person, instead, in a whiny,
obstinate voice, as if he's the final authority
on their experience.

* * *

Jen and I felt our time together slipping away. When we met for our first practice writing session, it was already the 18th of June. Jen was scheduled to leave town on July 6th. We had to make every minute count.

When the day for goodbyes arrived, we made this pact: to carry on our practice writing while Jen was on tour and swap our stuff whenever she had access to a friend's mailing address.

Practice writing and the supportive environment with Jen had worked something loose inside me. Monday, July 12—less than a week after saying goodbye to my dear friend and writing partner—I was buried in an avalanche of inspiration; the most intense landslide of inspiration in my entire history of wounded writing. The embryonic material for a book took me by storm, and I felt like I was hyperventilating in ideas. Panic set in. "Where do I start?" I was nervous I wouldn't be able to get it all down on paper before it melted and then evaporated.

Fear of writing, fear of failure, besieged me from every angle. "What if I can't do justice to the ideas in my head? What if I forget most of it, and I'm left with only the tattered remnants of a once-exciting vision? What if this project is too much for me? I might be taking on something I'm not really capable of. . . . "

To take a smaller bite of what was possible, I forced myself to do a practice writing session first. What had once seemed so daunting—less than a month ago over a mug of comforting latté with Jen—now seemed like the easy part. Had we really come so far in such a short time?

After allowing myself to be wild for thirty minutes within the safety of practice writing, I no longer felt as if I was going in cold. Ideas transferred themselves into my notebook without loss of blood, and the book was born.

Meanwhile, Jen and I kept our pact sporadically via mail. One amazing packet from Jen contained ten practice writing pieces, including two full-blown characterizations. It's like getting a birthday or Christmas present in the mail! In return, I wrote her a long letter about the avalanche and sent her some of my own practice writing pieces.

* * *

Almost three months later—after Jen gets back to Taos—we discover that somehow, even while in different parts of the country, we bought identical notebooks to use for practice writing. We eagerly make a date to meet in the sunshine at Peak Espresso and sit down to write. But we feel lost for a way to start.

We realize we are having a classic attack of "fear of practice writing," and we brainstorm until we come up with a topic: Santa Claus. We write about Santa Claus from two perspectives—Jen as the child and me as Santa. We each make a familiar speech about how hopeless our own story is, and then we look at each other and laugh. We swap our notebooks and, as usual, delight in what we read.

Once again, we're out wading together in the shark-infested waters of self-expression. Are we having fun yet?

Oui . . . Si Señor . . . Ja!

JEN SPEAKS

PRACTICE WRITING, SUNDAY, JUNE 20
by Jen

I used to love hanging out with my "artist" friends in college. In fact, most of them were art majors. I felt I could completely relate to their aesthetic values and sensibilities. But I was too terrified to sign up for even a beginner's art course. No, I had to be more "grounded" in college, or else it would appear to be frivolously wasting my dad's money for the tuition. But, if I'm really honest, I believe that I've always had an artist's heart and soul within my being. My grandmother would take my artwork from elementary school and frame it. I don't know why, but I always felt as though she took something from me when she did that. Maybe a sense of total abandonment and freedom of expression. I was once graded an A++ for a spontaneous charcoal drawing in the seventh grade. It was an indoor scene with a window that showed a winter mountain outside. Well, the teacher had put the grade on the back so as not to mar the drawing. When my grandmother snatched *the drawing from me and then gave it back framed, she had put—in red ink—an A++ on it in a conspicuous way. From then on, I felt too embarrassed to show it, because it seemed as though the grade made it worthy when actually I felt it ruined my innocent expression. Ever since then, I remain more of an observer in creative expression than a true participant. It's funny how I have followed my pattern from college and have spent the past thirteen years with an extremely open and creative artist . . . but I'm beginning to understand that exploring art in a safe and vicarious manner is no longer enough. There is energy inside that needs to be expressed, regardless of the validity or response it may provoke. Doing these exercises with Milli is helping me not to constantly edit every word or gesture I emit. I'm truly grateful for this time to blab, play, explore, vomit, cry, moan, cringe, laugh, coddle, exacerbate, sing, dance, just let the hand do its thing . . . <u>whatever</u>. Perhaps I'm retrieving a part of my soul that I'd relinquished as a child.*

FLIGHT OF THE WOODPECKER

To put it simply: Practice writing has become my path to inner salvation.

It's important for me to state up front that I didn't experiment with practice writing in order to facilitate a writing career. In fact, my previous experiences were limited to arduous, frantic college assignments that I would inevitably put off completing until the very last minute. I'm convinced I aged at least a year for every "all-nighter" I pulled off during those four years. And I always had the convenient excuse to tell my ego, if the paper wasn't given a top grade, that my efforts had been well received considering the small and rushed effort I'd invested to create it.

So when my dear friend Milli invited me to join her at practice writing, my first response was to run out of my front door and lock her inside the house! All I could think was that I had nothing clever or creative or eloquent to say. After all, I wasn't a *writer* and had never even secretly harbored a passion to write and publish my own material.

The mere notion of writing and then, God forbid, reading our words to each other was way beyond my comfort zone! All of my deep-seated fears instantly surfaced: I'm not smart or artistic; I'm lazy and boring and too self-conscious; I've got nothing worthy to say, and what would I say; I'm pseudo-bohemian—no, a wannabe bohemian. I'm a textbook codependent and would need to please every potential reader (imagined or real); furthermore, I'd be reliving my college Procrastination Queen title, etc.

Small wonder that I'd never been one for pursuing much in the way of artistic adventures. But the timing of Milli's proposition was crucial to my reluctantly acquiescing. Bottom line: I was literally sick and tired, after thirty-six years, of living with the constant voice of criticism playing continuously inside my mind—like a scratchy broken record. It was time for me to make a concerted effort to release those imprisoning and haunting phantoms from my past and to initiate a process of discovering . . . me.

* * *

That first practice writing meeting was, to be honest, a bit painful. I felt pretentious sitting in a coffeehouse with a notebook and pen, knowing I looked the part of a seasoned writer. But, I reminded myself, my intention was to open up; I wasn't there to impress anyone.

Milli and I spent two hours chatting about everything *else* under the sun except the "writing practice" we were supposed to attempt. I kept hoping maybe she would forget the original purpose of our meeting. I felt nervous and shaky; my inner child was frightened to death of impending judgment. But Milli shifted our focus and gently reminded me that the main purpose behind this exercise was to let the thoughts flow freely.

It was time to take my first baby steps into a whole new world free of limitations and "shoulds." This was not about striving for an "A" or wonderful reviews or outside validation. Practice writing would be the doorway to finally releasing those invisible creative shackles and learning to embrace spontaneity and playfulness; truly accepting myself at any given moment.

My first piece was constricted and self-conscious, but at least I *did* it and *shared* it! I was becoming a verb instead of only a noun!

The more I wrote during the following weeks the more free I became. I was experiencing a deeply personal initiation process. I felt myself stretch outwards physically, mentally and emotionally. I cherished the regular morning practice writing I gifted myself each day. My inner child, who had always cowered in fear and shame, began to blossom. She played and spoke and cried and danced and sang her Truth—at last.

* * *

The unfolding process continues. Practice writing is a life-line for me, guiding me out of a dark, cold and turbulent sea of emotional insecurity and self-doubt. Sometimes, as I reach another wave of exploration and expression, I panic and feel as though I might drown in a tidal wave of scrutiny and embarrassment. But, if I just hang on and allow the process to evolve with patience and tenderness, I find I'm able to ride the waves and enjoy the unexpected twists and turns of the surf.

As a result, practice writing is affecting my inner and outer vision and the way that I relate to the world.

Last week we found a woodpecker stuck in our wall. He pecked frantically, systematically chipping away the adobe, but he couldn't tear through the metal mesh supporting the wall. He eventually moved into the fireplace, where we could see him through the glass doors. We gently approached him, but he panicked and flew up the chimney. Then he returned to the cramped wall space and pecked away in desperation.

Our landlord's advice was to let him die in the wall. My heart ached with sadness and a sense of dread. I felt paralyzed with a hopeless depression. The next morning, I woke up to the same intense and frenzied sounds echoing through the house like a death knell. This bird had a strong and vital spirit and he was not about to give up. I felt that I must not give up either.

I made a prayer to the spirits of my departed pets. I'd never done this kind of ritual before, but I'm learning to trust and stretch the envelope. I asked them to communicate with the bird and let him know that we wanted to help free him from the wall.

I went downstairs and found him pecking furiously. I waited quietly and prayed. A minute later he hopped back into the fireplace. I walked up to him while he sat still. We stared into each other's eyes. I softly told him that we were going to set him free; his job was to momentarily let go of the fear and trust us and the Great Spirit. I told him that it might feel a bit scary—especially when we open the doors and my husband picks him up. He needed to understand this was his only route to freedom: The other option was certain death.

He slowly closed his eyes as though in an ecstatic trance. I called my husband over and told him the bird was ready. We opened the doors and, instead of trying to escape, the bird continued to sit quietly in an obvious state of surrender. My husband picked him up with a towel and took him through the house to our front door. He stepped outside to an open area and released the bird. The woodpecker flew fast and high. We felt a sense of exhilaration as if witnessing the flight of the soul upon death.

That bird was courageous. He put aside instinctive fears and let go to a situation which normally signaled danger. He chose a strange and foreign path in order to continue his life. Had he stayed with fear and rejected the scarier alternative, he'd have suffered a slow and painful death.

CHANTING THE DOUHM

PRACTICE WRITING, SATURDAY, JUNE 26
by Milli

A writer is someone who writes. No one can be a writer without the process of writing. I may want to be a writer, but if I don't write I can't develop. Then comes the question of quality: Am I good enough to be a writer? Jen's someone who believes she is not a writer yet I love to read her stuff. If someone else wants to read our stuff and they think it's fascinating and good, is that enough to make us writers? Can we do it without self-belief? What if I lived in a pure and noble society where writers were revered like gold. Where writers held a place in society as sacred as any priest. Where the people worship writers as the channel of creativity and the soul of expression. Would I be relegated to the wannabe pile? In my own society I remain an unpublished author. Even as I talk about this Utopian society, I long to create the image on paper of such an ideal place. Yet I stick with the dull realities of questioning my ability and speculating about "talent." What if I could transport this mundane practice writing to that place: create a well-adjusted society in a mythical land. What would it be called? It has to sound ethereal—cannot be another rotten apple à la New York City or L.A. It needs a magical name. Ordinarily, when inventing a name for a character or a place name for a make-believe setting, I would stop and ponder; jot down options, transpose letters or maybe look in magazines for inspiration. But the Natalie Goldberg rule for writing practice ("keep your hand moving") means I can't stop for that whimsical connection to my subconscious—a moment which might produce the perfect name. If I don't have a name for my society I have the perfect excuse not to put it on paper. How can I go forward without a name?

OK, Milli, just break the rules. Start a new page and give yourself the time you need to visualize and formulate. . . .

THE LAND OF IL RHANESIA

The land of IL Rhanesia shimmers in a haze of mountain sunshine. It is a land rooted in the ancient soil of Kavezh Daneel: a coastal range of gently undulating peaks, like the robed laps of giant mothers nursing precious bundles.

The capital city of IL Rhanesia, known to the people as Douhm (dow-oom), exists above and below ground. The buildings seen aboveground are changeable structures, and they are held in place by the vibration of intent expressed through sound. They linger in space unsupported by pillars or foundations.

The walls at first appear to be mosaics of beadwork the colors of the rainbow and more. The beadwork takes on a look of blossoming flowers; and then, as the eye shifts to drink in an elusive tint, appears in another dimension as rippling saffron fields of grain. The windows of the houses, delicately transparent screens of mother-of-pearl, draw the heart to scenes of inner life—as if viewing someone's most lyrical thoughts pantomimed in color, dance and song.

The ageless word "Douhm," pronounced with great reverence, is the tool the people use to keep their city held aloft. It is considered a special and coveted duty but is not restricted to the holy men or the seers. It's a gift treasured by every citizen and prepared for from the age of three.

People come to the chant center in a spontaneous flow. There are no rules or regulations; only revelations of the heart. Some may come heavily burdened by anxiety or sorrow and yet are not turned away. The tinge of suffering in their chanting is considered as vital as the chanting done with an attitude of joy.

The chant can take any form it is moved to take so long as the word "Douhm" is undercurrent. For instance, one day a man came in to chant while nursing a big grudge against his wife. Pyrgnüu, who is sorely frustrated that his wife counsels their daughter to leave home while only ŸÐ moons old, begins with a piercing "Yiyh-ah-naa" which has no meaning in the language but satisfies his urge to rant.

From a point miles away in a grassy meadow where the shepherd boy Zilb plays a reed flute to his flock, the city of Douhm can be watched undergoing its subtle shifts. Its structures are constantly evolving—taking on new textures, shapes and hues—but Zilb tunes to this shift in particular because his heart is involved. Pyrgnüu's daughter, Leianay, is the one he loves.

Zilb puts down his flute and watches as pink sparks appear, in a section of moving tapestry suggesting fragrant pines. The sparks seem to "plunk" with a brassy note which causes Zilb to grin. Something about the plunking suggests freedom and soaring—even though in itself can be read the energy of anger and possessiveness.

The pink sparks take on red centers of liquid light. They bob and pulsate in a fat and pleasing manner like a rain droplet ready to burst upon the soil. By now, Pyrgnüu is well into his lament. He knows he doesn't have to temper himself here in the chant room, and he puts his soul into expressing the sounds of his discontent. Around him, many are chanting Douhm. Some are using drumbeat to mimic the sacred syllables.

No one attempts to keep the beat or the chanting in harmony with anyone else, but the effect is not discordant. In fact, if there is one underlying rule of the Douhm chant it is that participants must do it on a personal level. It must be a true expression of each individual—not an attempt to fit in with others or learn to imitate another's style.

Pyrgnüu burrows deep within his emotion of anger. Within it, he finds many aspects of himself to vocalize. An irritated pride that doesn't want to let go of what belongs to the master of the house. A sense of powerlessness in the face of his wife's quiet insistence. Futility at the generation gap between father and daughter. But there's also a canny exuberance; delight in the power of his own sounds. It feels good to release his anger: cleansing and therapeutic.

In a surge of physical rejuvenation, his fingers and arms tingle and his breath seems to reach all the way to his toes. There is fear; a primal threat to his intactness. In his mental landscape, the saber of his wife's wisdom and sureness threatens to kill his confused ego. He feels forsaken by his own wisdom. At this lonely thought, Pyrgnüu's angry chant rises to a pitch and then breaks into sobs of regret.

As he grieves the loss of his little girl, his sobs become the chant: Douhm, Douhm. Leianay, once a dimpled lass playing in the woods, is now a woman with goals of her own. Finally, he admits (if only to himself): "I've kept her home too long using any lame excuse I could." Now even Pyrgnüu knows that his wife is right.

He has exhausted his anger and can deny nothing. Pyrgnüu lies on his side and recovers from the inner storm. He feels a connection with all those who chant.

He is still making sounds but gradually it becomes a chant of renewal. He looks inside and knows that he, too, possesses wisdom. He remembers the time when Leianay was only đ moons and had run away from home. Pyrgnüu had found a way to let her come home again without losing face. Later, when she was older and could analyze the experience, she thanked him for this fatherly gift.

Curled on his side, Pyrgnüu lets the Douhm become a new sound of self-affirmation. The pink sparks with the red kernels of pulsating energy also transmute to match his mood. At first, as he sobbed, the sparks were a curtain of colored rainfall slanting in the wind. Now the sparks meld into a gentle ocean suggesting tropical climes and comforting silence within a flow of water.

Zilb's grin broadens and he picks up his flute.

THE PASSIVE ZONE & THE ACTIVE ZONE: SHORT STORIES & EXERCISES

WORM MEDICINE

The Parakeet Café is thriving. The air smells of potato and leek soup and warm focaccia bread.

Narelle stops to admire the solo exhibition by a local Aboriginal artist on display in the alfresco section. The vivid dot paintings evoke primordial images of survival rooted in beauty and desolation. Tribal women foraging for witchetty grubs amid the roots of ancient trees. Early morning kangaroo hunts in the mist. The stark black and red of the bush fire tragedy. The startling, out-of-season yellow and red of wattle and waratah blossoming in the Blue Mountains snow.

Her silent vote for #1 uses precision yellow, black and white dots against an undulating, whorled series of olive and silver mosaic grids. Entitled *Cockatoo Dreaming*, the painting produces the effect of cockatoos flying through eucalyptus leaves blowing in a breeze. Narelle can feel the consummate artistry ripping her heart with an all-too-familiar, shattering claw of self-abomination.

She takes a seat and orders decaf cappuccino. Staring dismally at each table in turn, she plays her old college game of "Spot the Writer." A man eating unbuttered bread at the table beside her makes notes with his felt-tip in the margin of the newspaper propped against his soup bowl.

That doesn't prove he's a writer, she thinks.

But, it's no consolation. It never is.

As she sucks the cappuccino foam from her teaspoon, she watches the African drummer performing under colored spotlights on the tiny uncurtained stage. His sidekick, playing zills, is no more "African" than he is—but she's sinuous and exotic. Narelle envies them both with a hollow vengeance.

In her voluptuous, coin-chinking Middle Eastern costume, the dancer shimmies in a mystic desert mirage. Plying her finger cymbals in sync with a soulful barefoot stomp, she embodies the ultimate in passion and creative desire.

Why do I torture myself this way?

Narelle pays for her coffee and goes outside into the streaming Katoomba rain. She catches the mid-morning bus back to Leura and then walks home through the trickling fog settled thick and low over the outlying suburban hills. Flocks of shiny currawongs, amassed in the branches of the scribbly gums, give off an echoing, stereophonic warble. The vibrant rainsong echoes in her shriveled heart as sorrow and despair.

She feels, even smells, the majesty of the mountain scene with an agonized aestheticism; her natural perceptions married to a cruel, analytical, insidious inner presence—one which continually reminds her of her "imperfections." This gloating critic has reduced her creative awareness to a raw and weeping sore . . . instead of the gift of richness and joy she feels it truly ought to be.

When she reaches the bush line at the remote edge of town, Narelle is painfully aware of Damien's car sitting in her driveway; motor running and headlights on high beam. Spying on him from the summit of Craigend Street, she debates whether to surrender or escape.

At the corner of St. Andrews Place, she longs to go for the tranquility of the scenic path to Sublime Point Lookout. But the ever-gathering droplets of fog and the bone numbing Blue Mountains' chill make the scenic prospects dubious and the physical discomfort highly unappealing.

Something about this dreary day seems portentous. Shivering inside her R. M. Williams oilskin raincoat, Narelle totters carefully down the steep, pebbly and slippery perils of her high-altitude driveway. The fog clouds drip rain.

Damien greets her with a smile. "Did you forget?" he baits her gently.

She did forget their date. She glosses past the error by sliding in wordlessly when he opens the passenger door. She remains silent during the drive. Narelle hears the rainfall increase in tempo on the roof of the car as they pass the angular dome of the old Hydro Majestic hotel.

Despicable weather for a field trip, she mutters within the privacy of her brain. Damien hums to a sweeping classical piece on the radio. He seems inordinately pleased with himself—and with the day in general.

In Blackheath, at the traffic lights on Bundarra Road, they get off the Great Western Highway and cross the tracks at Blackheath Station. Damien swings left onto the Heritage route along the railway line. At the outskirts of Blackheath, they begin the heart-stopping descent to the Megalong Valley.

Narelle clings nervously to her seatbelt while Damien maneuvers the hairpin bends; albeit dependably and with an attitude of calm. The treacherous, rain-slicked road gradually gives way to dryer pavement as the tree line closes around them like a protective arm.

Down in the rainforest twilight, the rain is filtered to a mere drizzle. Seclusion and wildness bear down on them like a message from the universe. Narelle opens her window and takes in lungfuls of the crisp, creek-scented air.

"Stop here," she commands, pointing to an obscure turn-off along the narrow shoulder. Damien swerves expertly and comes to a glorious, sliding halt in the mud.

The sign in the parking lot reads "Mermaid Caves." Behind it, a National Parks and Wildlife walking track cuts through the enchanted old growth.

"Don't you want to fossick down in the valley as we agreed?" Damien asks her, a faint whine underpinning his question.

"No."

He starts to say, "Sweetheart, the driest rocks will be on the valley floor—" but she can predict his responses like a clock chiming the hour and is already out of the car. Damien follows her down the brooding, hypnotic track.

"Wait!" he calls. "Here are some amazing specimens already. They look heavy, too, so the closer we stay to the car the less strain it'll be on our spines."

Narelle looks at the bush rocks Damien is lusting for. Pale green lichen mottles the upper regions in delicate snowflake storms. The rocks' lower quarters—hunkered in clear creek water burbling from a hidden spring—wear petticoats of emerald moss waving in the current.

"I don't need them," she says.

"But, honey, they'd be perfect for your rock garden," he persists.

It would be a crime to uproot these rocks from their sacred forest home. How can she get that across to someone as dogged and prosaic as Damien?

"It's cruel to move them," she states with tight control.

"But this was the entire reason we came down here," Damien protests. "To look for some authentic bush rocks to landscape your garden."

"That was your idea."

Damien cocks a look at her. "So?"

Narelle feels something horrible and furious flaming in her chest.

"Why do you work overtime to try to please me?" she yells. "Do you know how suffocating it is?"

She can feel herself starting to shriek.

Damien stares. "What's this, Nell? I've never seen you act this way before."

His obtuseness stokes her fury afresh. And she always hates it when he calls her Nell. She feels positively violent, but she stays put next to a mossy tree fallen diagonally across the creek. Rather than pummeling his stubborn, bone-headed frown—or pushing him backward into the creek—she opens her mouth and starts to scream. It's less a scream than a frustrated roar; rough, painful and hoarse. Damien backs away from her.

"You've lost it, girl," he says.

Narelle keeps it coming. She's doubled over now; contorted in the effort of releasing her torrent of what amounts to . . . powerlessness.

It isn't even about Damien any more. In fact, he's the last thing on her mind. When she sinks to the forest floor and tries to catch her breath, it takes her a moment to remember where she is. Damien's nowhere to be seen. Above her ragged breathing, she can hear the car's motor running.

She walks unsteadily to the entrance of the soggy path and gets into the car. Damien pulls out of the cutaway to begin the drive home. Not a word is spoken all the way back to Hester Road. The atmosphere in the car is so tense and full of mutual rejection, Narelle longs to bail out and hit the highway rolling. As soon as Damien comes to a stop in her driveway, she catapults herself out the door.

Damien rolls down his window.

"You should get yourself a job!" he snaps. "You need something constructive to do with yourself." Then drives off.

Narelle feels too inwardly scoured to get furious with him again. *Is that the best he can do? Even his insults are mediocre.*

A moment later her mind is focused on the real issue. She enters the house and goes to her desk. The manuscript, she knows, is sitting in the third drawer. She pulls it out and examines her most recent addition. Across the bottom margin, in red pen, she has scrawled: "Editor's verdict: slush!"

She hugs the pages to her chest and takes them with her into the bedroom. The curtains are drawn and it's a dim, overcast afternoon but she doesn't turn on a light. In front of the mirror, in the gloom, Narelle faces herself and tries a last-ditch, self-assured smile—which only makes things worse. She can't stand what she sees.

"I despise you!" she shouts. "You useless, non-event blah. You don't even make it as ugly! Just good ol' plain and mousy. Insipid. Dull. You're beyond nothing into Quantum Nothing. Wishy-washy-in-between. Boring. Mundane. A hack writer—trite and clichéd—with less zing than a worm!"

She heaves this out with all the venom she can muster. Maybe she can kill herself with sheer verbal poison.

But—as she stands shouting and looking herself in the eye—from some wretched, low-down place Narelle catches a hint of self-compassion and begins to weep. She barely has the energy to let it out, but once the tears are flowing the intensity takes over and guides her to the truth. In the midst of wrenching sobs, she finally knows what it is. It's that voice.

When she's done crying and can blow her nose, she looks in the mirror again and this time the smile is sincere.

"It's not really me hating me," she marvels out loud. "The voice is not me."

The inward defect—which has been with her as long as she can remember—can now be examined in a new light. The voice of criticism, self-hatred, failure and lassitude comes from somewhere outside of her: an implant; a microchip of self-destruction. Now that she knows it doesn't belong to her essential self, she wonders how she can separate the wheat from the chaff.

An idea takes hold.

Narelle stuffs a few items into a leather backpack. She stands on her porch and locks the back door, gets into her poor, beaten-up 1980 Datsun, and looks at her watch.

Good thing it's still relatively early, she thinks, taking the steep incline of the wet driveway gingerly in first gear.

Crossing the railway bridge on her way out of Leura, she hooks a left onto the Great Western Highway. It takes her almost forty-five minutes driving northwest to reach the Bells

Line of Road at Bell. From there, she follows the gravel track through the dripping State Forest for another thirty-five kilometers of concentrated thought.

At Bungleboori Picnic Reserve she stops to drink from the spigot: Her instinct to stop is rewarded with a glimpse of swamp wallabies loping gracefully through the undergrowth. The fog-swathed cathedral of eucalyptus trees echoes with the harsh call of magpies defending their young from the sudden threat of human contact.

When she gets back in the car, she returns to pondering the invisible, leeching energy of her nefarious alter ego. By the time she reaches Deane's Siding, Narelle is getting tired of the muddy, rutted conditions. At the isolated pioneer junction on Old Coach Road, she feels a churning of tummy butterflies as she nears her goal.

Upon reaching the Information Shelter for Wollemi National Park, Narelle gets out of her car to judge the light.

Better not walk in, she decides.

The long, lonely, primeval bushwalk would have been in perfect keeping with her intent, but the afternoon is progressing. She doesn't want to be caught in there in the dark, alone. She drives another four kilometers to the deserted vehicle barrier and shuts off her engine. Grabbing her bottled water and backpack, she dons a cotton-lined windcheater unearthed from the junkyard on the back seat.

In a light, misting rain, she undertakes the final kilometer of her pilgrimage to Bell's Grotto on foot. Hidden rock warblers give intermittent bursts of song. Narelle visualizes them somewhere in the leaf litter—happily splashing in rain puddles and fluffing their feathers like a ritual in a fairyland health spa.

The ruins of the Wolgan Valley Railway lend an eerie, abandoned undertone to the walk. There is no one else on the track with her: She freezes at a sudden rustling and then feels an adrenalin rush when the birdcall comes.

Lyrebirds! She peers in the direction the sounds came from but can see only bushes, trees, and rain-streaked rock formations. Drizzle gathers on her eyelashes as she waits in suspense. The birds remain concealed in the trees; alert to her presence. Narelle moves on slowly, disappointed.

When she reaches the tunnel, she slows her pace even further and makes each footstep reverent. Bell's Grotto, affectionately known as the Glow Worm Tunnel, is alive with the blue gleam of a multitude of insect larvae. Narelle drinks in the bioluminescence like manna from the gods.

She notices the voice going wild. "Shut up!" she tells it, and then puts down her backpack on the only rock shelf that doesn't look utterly awash in mud.

Ducking and dodging carefully so as not to dislodge the delicate squirming larvae with her thick, curly hair, she opens her backpack and takes out her pocket torch. She unscrews the bulb cap, replaces the AA batteries, then switches it on and rests it against the rock at an acute angle. The torch gives her a tiny pool of light to work by.

Removing her manuscript from the backpack, Narelle scrabbles at the bottom of the bag looking for a pen. As her fingertips brush against a small glass tube, inspiration strikes. She pulls it out and squints at the lettering on the side of the tube with the help of the narrow torch beam.

"Celtic Blend," it reads. "Fine Essential Perfume Oils."

Narelle tries to read the name of the scent on the lid, but all she can make out is the black Stonehenge symbol on the faded silver label. She remembers that the bottle might once have contained lavender roll-on perfume. She removes the lid and sets it on the rock beside her. The plastic roller-ball is limp and floppy in its moorings: She bites it out gently and spits it onto her palm.

Next, she picks up the dog-eared manuscript. Narelle displays it to her captive audience, the glow worms, like a midwife holding up a newborn babe.

"With the glow worms as my solemn witness," she intones, "I hereby acknowledge the existence of my creativity."

Narelle speaks quietly—having learned that the larvae are sensitive creatures liable to asphyxiate on a whiff of car exhaust or perish at a human touch. Hefting the glass tube in her free hand, she holds it aloft. Like a priestess in an ancient sacramental cave, she tilts her head back and journeys deep within her heart.

Once she locates the crawling, seething mire of anti-life, she takes a breath and mentally draws it to the surface. Bending forward in a slight curve over her left hand, and with a controlled, steady exhale through pursed lips, she blows the spirit of the voice into the tube.

In one quick switch, Narelle throws down the manuscript and grabs the bottle cap. She screws it on briskly to avoid leaving any traces lurking in the tunnel.

Relief and energy flood her limbs. She tries to think of some ceremonial words to speak over the tube. All she can think of, at first, is a Louis Armstrong quote she'd seen once in a book: "What we play is life."

After organizing her thoughts, she holds the tube at arm's length and tunes her senses to the mass of blue tresses pulsating softly in the murk.

"The voice and I were not designed to coexist," she states. "It has been a massive waste of precious life force. Perhaps apart, we can each find our own way to resonate truth. Whatever the truth may be."

A pile of rotting leaf litter, blown into a niche in the tunnel wall on the wings of the mountain wind, is the only available burial ground. Narelle squats and burrows the tube into the warm, moist bed of compost.

"Let the voice rest here, undisturbed, forever."

Brushing debris from her hands, she rises and makes a humble curtsey in honor of the glow worms.

Leaning against the rock shelf momentarily, Narelle

realizes there is still some unfinished business. Her cheeks flush with a mixture of amusement and embarrassment: picturing herself at home earlier that day blasting vile insults at the mirror, comparing herself to the clichéd lowliness of the earthworm.

She murmurs with her head bent low in respect: "I'm sorry I underestimated you as a species."

The glow worms writhe in communal forgiveness.

"There's an apology due to another worm in this dark and stormy tale," Narelle says, with a cheesy, lopsided grin. She chokes up with emotion and adds in a halting whisper: "I'm sorry I underestimated you—I mean, me."

Wrapping both hands across her heart, she lets the healing tears run.

FERTILE MATERIAL

YIN & YANG You've just had the worst year of your life. Go ahead and list the disasters, the betrayals, and the disappointments. You kept your chin up for the first eleven months, but now it's Christmas—a time of "good cheer"—and you're mad, bad, and ready to break things. You're sick and tired of being told to look on the bright side and "find the silver lining."

HOW MANY KARATS? Your 13-year-old son, Beldon, has been given a special Family Communications assignment by his Social Studies teacher, Mrs. Feinbone. Your family must observe silence together for one full day. Describe the family. Instead of using your voices, how will you communicate? Is silence really golden? Each family member must write a paragraph to be included in Beldon's report.

SOLITAIRE ISLAND You are the lighthouse keeper on an unpopulated island a few miles offshore. You communicate with the mainland via shortwave radio and write long letters to your friends. There's no television, Internet, or DVD. Once a month you go ashore for supplies and socializing. How do you feel about being so isolated? What's it like to go ashore when you are not accustomed to urban living? Do you have family on the island? What do you think about during the lonely hours? How do you keep yourself entertained? When friends visit, is it fun? . . . Or do they find it dull, dull, dull; incessantly moaning: "How do you cope out here month after month? I'd go ballistic!"

THE GOD OF MYSTERY

My ex-wife, Dory, sits on the sofa in my Greenwich Village apartment looking wet around the eyes. Beside her sits a stack of diaries—the kind with golden locks and two miniature keys strung on red thread. The cover of the one she's reading has a panda bear with a raised velveteen nose. The forlorn panda clutches a drooping sunflower with velveteen petals. The colors are lurid and childish.

"Have you read these yet?" Dory implores, with a melodramatic sob.

"I've got a deadline," I tell her. It's irritating to have to state the obvious.

"Oh, brother," she says. "You're so far ahead of that deadline it's obscene. You could write those things in your sleep by now, Sean."

The woman has a nerve. Dory's never written anything more complex than a shopping list. What would she know about the terrors of deadlines?

"Anyway," she pipes, "you embarrass Spence when you submit them too early."

Dory is doing her yabbering act again. I'm deep into emergency revision on a crucial section of Chapter Eleven: the lead-up to revealing "whodunit." My editor, Spencer J. Harwood, has suggested I tie in a clue from Chapter Seven. I need to find the perfect spot to work it in. It isn't like me to miss a clue or forget to include one in the wind-up. Good thing this is my last book.

"Dory, why don't you shut up and let me write. No

wonder we got divorced. I could never get any work done around here—what with your constant harping about nothing and your mindless chatter about the latest shade of lipstick."

"We're divorced because you didn't give me enough sex," Dory says calmly, and then goes back to her reading.

I deftly ignore the bait as it screams and wriggles on the hook.

Dory has married and divorced twice since we split. Her latest boyfriend is a retired flight engineer with a red sports car. I know she's thinking of dumping him.

"He's good in bed but that's about it," she is inordinately fond of stating. And this from a seventy-two year old grandmother.

For thirty-eight years, this brazen woman drove me crazy with her rampant libido. It was an unspeakable relief to become single and celibate again, even though it cost me dearly. Dory took me to the cleaners as the saying goes: the house, the car, the kids, the furniture, the pots and pans—the whole shebang.

We've been divorced now for fifteen years, but I've never truly been rid of her. Even during her second and third marriages she considered it her God-given privilege to infringe on my time, deliver preachy editorials on my "tame" love life, and make it her business to "critique" my manuscripts. As if Dory, of all people, would know a single thing about the process of writing mysteries!

Strangely enough, Spencer religiously asks for—and even appears to value—her opinion. Oh, well. Even the best men have their blind spots.

"You know," Dory starts up again, "there's only one Norse god missing from your books. It's become a glaring omission, Sean. What's wrong with Bragi, god of poetry? You've used his wife, Idunn. You've used Njord twice, and Thor gets to star in almost every book. Weland the Craftsman is into overkill with his clever tools, and Gefion has taken so many virgins the poor thing is yawning from boredom. Only Bragi has been left out in the cold."

"Bragi is a wimp," I inform her tartly. "Everyone knows Cagney would never identify with a guy who writes poetry—god or no god. Bragi doesn't fit the genre."

My most popular and enduring mystery series features the detective, Cagney Thoreau: an amateur expert on Norse gods and their mythology. Thoreau takes on crimes assigned to the "too hard" basket. He solves each case by analyzing clues through the omnipotent mind of a Norse god; usually a different god in each book.

He gets so involved in his cases, he is like one of those Hollywood method actors who lives the character off-screen as well as on. For the duration of the case, Cagney "becomes" a god; taking on the mythology and thriving on the adrenalin of fatalism, destiny, and power. When you can be Fafnir the Dragon or Vidar, Slayer of the Wolf, who needs poetry?

"You're chicken shit," Dory sniffs.

"What?"

The blood pressure takes a dive in my cholesterol-encrusted veins. I brace myself for a recital of my faults.

"You're scared to death of poetry," she trumpets. "It's too much like the dangers of art for your comfort."

"Don't be ridiculous," I laugh, relieved that this silly issue will be the full throttle of Dory's character assassination for the evening. "Poetry's too weak to be art."

"I know you inside out, Sean Dugan." Dory nods sagely, emanating smugness. "You have been in denial for forty years working to your precious formula; pretending that you only write for the money. If Kvasir was here in the room with us, he would tell you you've squandered the best years of your life hiding from your fears. You should do some *writing* one of these days, Mr. Typecast Detective—

before you kick the bucket and it's too late."

Kvasir is the Norse god of wise utterances. Dory has a bad habit of borrowing the gods to provide the morals for her insufferable sermons. The gospel according to Dory Denderholm . . . what a pain in the patootie.

"You know what, Dory?" I spin around on my ergonomic chair and pin her with my WWII glass eye. "I have written more copy and produced more manuscripts in forty years than you've had hot dinners. Don't *you* tell *me* to do some writing! I could've written an extra ten books before I retired—if only you would have SHUT UP AND LET ME CONCENTRATE!"

Dory rolls her eyes.

"Hallelujah. Ten more Cagney Thoreaus to enrich the minds of Cagney addicts and monopolize more space on the library shelves. Big deal, Daddy-o. Why don't you do something groundbreaking this time and write the teenage mother book for Jade? She's counting on you, you know."

Jade: our eighteen-year-old granddaughter and the mother of three-year-old Troy. When Jade turned twelve, I gave her a diary for her birthday. From that day forth, she has faithfully cluttered volume after volume with her girly talk and emotional trifles.

During Jade's fifteenth year, she became pregnant and gave birth to Troy. By that time, journaling was second nature to her. Even during the actual birth she continued to record her thoughts. In the labor ward, Dory sat beside Jade mopping her sweaty brow and transcribing her every word—in between coaching Jade's breathing and feeling faint at the sight of the painkiller needle Jade refused to submit to. That Jade is one stubborn girl.

My granddaughter recently broke the gold lock on her twenty-seventh volume. Those poor locks never survive her ardent dedication. Jade's got the gumption to write her own book . . . she doesn't need me.

"This is my last book," I remind my ex-wife, gesturing at the computer screen. "I'm retiring, remember? I've slogged my guts out for fifteen years beyond the average working life. I'm tired of the grind. Sick of the nine-to-five routine."

"My point, exactly."

Dory straightens her spine and smoothes her skirt like a graduate from etiquette school. She's really warming to her theme now. I know the telltale signs. She's going to sit there on her soapbox until hell freezes over.

"Retirement is for hobbies and other interests," she spouts. "Creative interests you didn't have time for during your career. Like writing a book based on something real for once. Not another market-driven formula with a lead character you practically sleep with."

"Writing is not creative, Dory" I explain wearily, as if talking to a forgetful child. "It's just another job; a nine-to-fiver. Any writer who tells you otherwise is nothing but a literary snob."

"You're such a pinhead, Sean," Dory says wearily, as if forced to state the obvious.

I raise my eyebrow in an indulgent question mark. It seems the flight engineer has been teaching Dory some modern lingo. Her current dye job is a twenty-something's brassy shade of blond. She's getting hipper every day. Her boy toy this time is only fifty-nine. . . . I suspect this latest stint of cradle robbing has gone to her head. Dory always was the vain type.

"Thanks so much for your unqualified opinion," I tell her. "Now I'll know which expert to come to if I'm ever in need of Geriatric Hobbies advice. Now, good night and good riddance."

Predictably, Dory leaves in a huff. Ah, alone at last.

* * *

Dear Diary,

Gramma Dody was wearing a new outfit yesterday. Her boyfriend Lionel was taking her to a new play on Broadway. Dody's so sweet. She's trying to get grumpy Grampa Sean to read my diaries. She says she just finished reading them from cover to cover, and she balled almost all the way through.

I don't want Gramma to be sad or to feel sorry for me for the rest of my life. But it is definitely nice to have her understanding. She's the only one who has been totally cool about what's happened.

Even when I first told her about my pregnancy, she didn't freak out or try to lay a trip on me. She asked me how I felt and what I wanted to do. She said if I was confused, I should hold off making my decision and not let other people influence me with their agendas. She told me she would support any decision I made.

It was still very difficult. Gramma wasn't around very much at that time—her second husband had gone to Spain and she was furious. She wanted to get the divorce, but he wouldn't come home from Madrid.

Meanwhile, everyone was trying to tell me what I should do. Even Mom. Mom's pretty cool for a mom, but she grew up in the hippy generation so she still tends to think abortion and feminism is the answer to everything. I think abortion is fine—the women who do need to do it should always have that choice. I just knew I couldn't.

I was so scared. And everyone was in my face. Now that Troy's three I can look back and see how screwed up I almost got by listening to other people's truths. Even though I made my own decision in the end, their "do-this-Jade, do-that-Jade" messages still play like tapes in my head.

I had four different counselors—but, would you believe it? Not one of them had ever been pregnant! What I really needed was somebody my own age who had been through it all before me. There is always some adult who can tell you your "options." They call it "making an informed choice." But there was nobody who could tell me how it actually FELT to make one of those choices.

I have a gut instinct saying it should be me who changes that. I've got you—the diaries—to help me tell the story. I've got it all on paper, now it should be shared. I want others out there to have what I didn't have—to have what I needed: a companion from the same nightmare but not from the same point in the dream. A companion who is awake again; who can get to the heart of the matter and help interpret the dream.

I want my book to speak to the ones who really need it. I want it to be a classic: the one Marie Claire *or* Cosmopolitan *will recommend.*

Grampa Sean says he's not the one I should look at if I insist on using a ghostwriter. He says I should write it myself. But my Grampa is so famous. His name on my

*book would make it an instant hit. Besides,
I am not an organized writer. I wouldn't
know which sections to put where. Only a
professional writer like Sean Dugan would
know that.*

*Grampa's just being a shit. Gramma
Dody says he's facing a demon. I'm not sure
what she means . . . except for some reason
Grampa is running away. I wish he would
grow up!*

* * *

When I wake up, I remember I'm wearing the boxer shorts
my daughter, Lydia, gave me for Christmas. They're tur-
quoise silk. An audacious image of Daffy Duck struts from
hem to hem sporting a loud and tasteless Bugs Bunny tie.
Silk boxers make me sweat.

I woke myself up on purpose because I was having a
bad dream. Usually I can lucid dream—control my actions
and mold the outcome—but this dream would not cooperate. This dream was unhealthy, so I pulled myself out of it
and woke myself up.

In the dream, I'm naked and sitting under an apple
tree in a meadow. I'm working on my manuscript and time
is running out for me. . . . I can see the sand running swiftly
in a giant hourglass. Idunn, goddess of the golden apples of
youth, perches on a giant toadstool and weighs one of her
famous apples in her upturned palm. I'm annoyed: She is
ruining my concentration; distracting me from my work.
She smiles and winks as if she knows something scrump-
tious that I don't know.

I tell Idunn her husband Bragi is really the god of
superfluous nonsense. Poems are for puppy love and for

intellectuals living in ivory towers. Intellectuals who think they see something "deep" in a few lines of posturing imagery. I tell her that writing is for entertaining the masses or for the dissemination of knowledge; nothing more. And writing can be for earning your bread and butter—not for lofty illusions of the heart. I tell her I'm about to complete another manuscript so I can get a paycheck for my words. My fans insist on formula. If I deviate from the formula my income will go down the tubes.

Idunn puckers her lips in amusement as if I've said something supremely silly. She opens her mouth wide and takes a bite of the apple. I can hear the crunch of her teeth breaking the golden skin and sinking into the juicy flesh. Her spittle, mixed with the heavy moisture of the apple, sprays in every direction. The spray hits me in both eyes and I am blinded. I cannot see my manuscript.

As I grope for a handkerchief to wipe the goddess saliva from my eyes, Idunn laughs and jabbers something in her native tongue. I strain my senses to figure out what she is saying. Idunn refuses to translate. That's when I pull myself out of the dream.

I lie in bed and look at the clock. It is a little after four a.m. My granddaughter Jade used to climb into my lap when she was little and pick my brains. "Tell me a dream, Grampa," she'd command, in her imperious, four-year-old style. I would close my eyes, find my center, and then tell her my best lucid dream from the night before.

Thirty-five years ago, I taught myself this artisan's skill. I use it religiously every night to develop story lines and spawn clues for my star detective. Once Jade heard one of my lucid dreams, she would never again settle for a sappy picture book or a juvenile nursery rhyme.

Jade has always been precocious. And now she has a three-year-old to take care of when she's still navigating childhood herself. Jade is obsessed with writing a book about her experiences as a teenage mother. What good will that do her? She will never recapture those lost years. It's a fruitless noble cause. Other girls her age are not going to listen or heed her cautionary tale—no one listens at that age. But Jade won't let it be. She's been pestering me for almost a year to be her ghostwriter. I tell her I don't write exposés. I tell her, "Take it to *The National Enquirer*. They love that kind of stuff."

Dory says, "*Ai yi yi!* What a sour old man. Can't you say something constructive to the poor girl?"

I get out of bed and go to my desk. Spencer has forwarded another ridiculous packet of fan mail for my so-called "enjoyment." I pick up the first letter; it is written in a crooked, masculine hand on tacky lavender notepaper.

Dear Mr. Dugan,

You're my all-time favorite mystery writer. I have read every Cagney Thoreau you've ever written at least three times each. My brother wrote a stage play for The God of Ships *and I starred as Cagney solving the crime using the wisdom of the god, Njord. We performed it at the summer theater festival here in Gladesville and sold out every night for a week. I am very sad that you're retiring. . . .*

I throw down the letter. My fans are obsessive people: Some of them think Cagney's a real person. They ask if they can meet him for lunch or get his autograph. They overnight him his favorite brand of cigar. A cattle rancher in Dixicana, Texas, sends a gilt-edged sleigh scene card every year like clockwork; formally inviting Cagney Thoreau to spend Christmas with his family "down home."

Spencer wants me to answer the mail and humor their whims, but I despise this sort of fantasy. People need to get a grip on reality—not be encouraged in their folly!

Sometimes, when I think of how I make my living pandering to fools, I get disillusioned. I designed Cagney to be a man of style and intelligence not a hero to middle class neurotics.

I wander away from my desk to make some coffee. While it perks, I sit on the couch drawing a blank. I need to solve this one last crime so I can put the workaholic Cagney Thoreau to bed once and for all.

Ordinarily, my system is flawless. Before I start the first draft, I write a synopsis and every clue is in place. The mystery is already solved on paper. All I have to do is write according to the master plan.

But this time I couldn't swing it. I laid the ground-work in the synopsis and had my ending roughed out as usual. Unfortunately, by the time I was eight chapters into the first draft, I knew my predetermined ending wasn't go-ing to work. I yelled at Spencer on the phone but that was no help; not even a decent target for my umbrage. He was gracious and said he knew I'd "come through" as always.

"You are a consummate writer, Sean," he purred at me. "You can write anything."

I hung up in his ear at that point. When I am in a pinch, I don't need a sycophant: I need a taskmaster. Now, Dory likes to think she's the voice of the conscience I'm too "mule-headed" to let myself have—my term for it is nag. If she knew something about writing I might listen, but she only knows how to read those trashy women's magazines. And she's always coming back from the bookstore with the next "Great American Novel."

I tell her there's no such thing. Novels are not "art"; merely self indulgence on the part of the writer. *Ai yi yi!*

That's when she always storms out of the room.

Good riddance, I always say.

Under a throw pillow I've been kneading, my hand bumps something with a blunt corner. I realize I'm sitting in the sublime presence of the first twenty-six volumes of Jade's diary. I extract one from under the pillow and flip it open to a random page. From the vital statistics, I can tell immediately that this particular volume is three years old.

Dear Diary,

Troy Andrew Fischer was born at 3:12 a.m. on Thursday, May 15, weighing 7 lbs and 2 ounces. He is 20 inches long and has a wet-looking patch of black hair that stands on end like fuzz on a baby monkey. Troy inherits his dark hair from his father, Mike, not from me. He sucks his thumb already; one day old. Mike was there for the entire labor. After the birth, he was cuddling Troy with tears streaming down his face. There in the labor ward, Mike asked me to marry him but I said no. We don't love each other that way—it's only because he wants to be Troy's dad. I told him he can still be a good dad; we don't have to be married for that.

Atrocious mushy stuff. I skip to the last page.

Dear Diary,

I have never been so tired in my whole life. Troy won't settle at night, and he will only take forty-five minute naps during the day.

He cries a lot, and the mothercraft nurse says he might have colic. Sometimes, I just sit down and cry with him.

Yesterday, I took Troy to the school to show him off to my friends. It took me two hours to get us both ready, but finally I strapped him to my ribs in the backwards backpack thing Mom gave me when he was born. Just as we were leaving, he vomited milk all over his new baby suit and I had to unstrap him and change him from head to foot. I had to change my clothes, too. My shoulders are always wet with baby drool and milk curds.

When we finally made it to school, it was almost last bell. Everyone cooed and fussed over my beautiful baby boy—even Principal Sedgwick came down to see us. He couldn't get over Troy's tiny fingers and toes. He said it brings tears to his eyes.

My English teacher, Mr. Crabtree, says I have more courage in my pinkie than he does in his whole body. What a sweetie.

My friends act as if Troy is a doll to play with, and they have no idea what I'm going through. I even miss school! Some days, I'm sure I'm going crazy. . . . But I do know I made the right decision. Troy is a precious gift of life.

I slam the diary shut. That English teacher, Mr. Crabtree, is a nosy do-gooder who should learn to mind his own damn business.

No doubt encouraged by Dory, Jade has tried one

ploy after another to convince me to ghostwrite her book of propaganda on the issues of teenage motherhood. She is so sure she's some kind of modern pioneer—says she "owes it" to the teenagers of our nation. I tell her to get over her martyr complex; it doesn't become her.

By far the most pitiful ploy was the time she sent me the fancy letter pretending to be a literary agent. The agent, "Saul Eisenbaum," promised a lucrative publishing deal if I would agree to write Jade's book. Saul's grammar stank, and the attached "agreement" was a parody of legalese that only a naïf like Jade could dream up.

Over the past year, Jade has attempted to soften me up with boxes of candy, movie passes, CDs, books, an expensive paisley silk necktie and an engraved silver fountain pen. Once, she even gave me a bottle of Chivas Regal and a heavy-bottomed crystal scotch glass to go with it. In each instance of bribery, Jade researched my tastes and came up with something to my exact liking.

I kept everything: consumed the chocolates and the whiskey; saw the movies; read the books; and listened to Rachmaninov on rainy afternoons. I used the fountain pen to sign autographs at the book launch for *God of the Sun* while wearing the paisley silk tie. They both went perfectly with the garnet and silver tiepin I inherited long ago from my father's meager, but tasteful, estate.

When Jade asked me if her presents had melted my "mean old Scrooge's heart," I told her to use the ingenuity she demonstrates at shopping to write the book herself.

Dory was beside herself with an attack of righteous indignation.

"*Ai yi yi!* Your big chance in life to do something decent, and you're as stingy as a dog with a bone. I hope Nemesis finds a sticky ending for you!"

As usual, whenever Dory's up in arms with me she trots out her trusty retinue of gods. Norse, Greek, Roman, or Egyptian—it's all the same to her.

"Better Nemesis than death by nagging," I tell her.

Another ploy which really backfired on Jade was to bring in Kevin Crabtree. Crabtree, Jade's former English teacher, has digested the first twenty-six volumes of Jade's diaries and declares them a work of art. He knows of her desire to have her precious book ghostwritten, and he also knows she has *me* targeted as the dumb bunny who's supposed to ghostwrite it for her. Put two and two together and what do you get? More of Jade's dirty work.

So, the noble-browed Mr. Crabtree called me on the telephone one fine day; ostensibly to discuss the "potential of the project." He talked about writers having the courage to demystify taboos and about Jade's ability to bring some "plain talk" to a subject riddled with adult jargon. He purported to have unlimited respect for my career and to be a fan of Cagney's. But his real reason for calling was obvious: More guilt tactics to get me to change my mind and say yes to Jade.

"The statistics in the USA are truly overwhelming," Crabtree expounded. "The problem of teenage pregnancy is growing worse, not better. We assume that kids are better informed in this day and age, but our girls still fall into the same traps they fell into in the '60s and '70s. They end up making the same choices: adoption, abortion, or drop out of school to raise the child. Jade's a saint . . . the rare victim who sees the bigger picture not just her own dilemma. The wealth of material she provides through her diaries should go down in posterity. Jade speaks for generations of girls who could learn to empower themselves with knowledge: to be aware of their choices in life *before* it ever comes to a life-altering decision. Or simply to feel they have a friend out there who understands if they *do* face such a decision. If Jade's book is published, I will personally see to it that every student in my English class receives a copy—boy, girl, or otherwise. This book will sweep the schools like a revolution. It's what these kids crave most—someone from their own world telling it like it is."

Crabtree was calling smack-dab in the middle of my afternoon writing session. Moreover, I did not take kindly to his breathy "passion" or busybody brand of idealism.

"My dear, dear Mr. Crabtree," I told him, in my best imitation of the English gentleman with the ol' plum in the mouth. "Go soak your head in a bucket." Then I hung up.

Next, I dialed Jade.

"Now, you listen to me, Miss Joan of Arc. I don't care how much you want to liberate humanity or bring the light of truth to your sisters nationwide. I am not going to write that book of yours, so you'd better learn to swallow the bitter pill. And if that Crabtree jerk ever calls me again, I'll go to his classroom and deal with him in person. Now, you'd better come and get these sniveling diaries out of my sight or I'll put them in the fire."

Jade was blubbering by the time I hung up. Predictably, Dory called me ten minutes later to give me the usual guff about my "lack of heart."

"Ah, it's you that has no heart," I point out. "You keep encouraging her to lobby for this when you know I'm going to reject her every time. I am sick of people claiming virtue in their selfish motives. You've been trying to prove a point to me for the past twenty years, and now you're dashing poor Jade on the rocks of your own pigheadedness."

Whenever I rise up and make an indisputable point, my empirical method ex-wife—Dory Denderholm, Mistress of Debate, ha!—conveniently seems to lose interest in the mechanics of argument.

"Your day will come," she proclaims as a diversion, nodding that nod of hers and trying to sound ominous.

Some people live under perpetual self-deception. Sadly, Dory has never been able to crack the psychology of meddling: that interfering in other peoples' lives is not a substitute for self-fulfillment. It's just a hobby to pass the time until you die.

* * *

It has been about a month since Crabtree's miscalculated pitch for Jade the Saint and teenage females everywhere. The bribery has stopped and so has the collusion from the "Pretty-*please*-write-Jade's-book-for-her" camp.

Even Dory put a sock in it and learned to avoid the subject. The boneheads who couldn't take no for an answer for almost a year finally conceded defeat. As far as I'm concerned, the matter's over and done with. But—wouldn't you know it?—Jade calls this afternoon with a brand new ploy.

"Grampa," she says urgently. "I'm giving a talk this evening at a Lamaze class for under-20s, and my babysitter had to cancel. I've called everyone in my address book, but no one is available. Please take care of Troy for me tonight, just this once."

"Not on your life," I tell her.

Chapter Eleven is not revealing its mysteries to me and I've had one helluva day. I have been on the phone to Spencer a dozen times, but he has been about as effective as the dust balls under my oak four-poster—delivering his usual platitudes and his simplistic, rousing speeches about his undying faith in my abilities.

"Grampa, PLEASE."

"Where's that wastrel of a father when you need him?" I demand. "He should be the obvious choice."

"Mike's out of town with his basketball team. They are playing in Musketville tonight."

"Then tell him to come back."

"Grampa," she says, with a tired sigh. "Mike's on a contract. He can't just walk away from a game."

"Well, *I* have a contract and a work commitment of my own. I have a deadline to meet and many pages to write before the job is done. Get your giddy grandmother to take the baby."

"Troy is not a baby anymore, Grampa," Jade says hotly. "He's three years old, and he doesn't need his diaper changed anymore. That's why I thought you might agree to do it just this once. He's much easier to take care of now. Gramma Dody has an appointment she can't break, otherwise she'd be more than happy to spend time with Troy."

"What appointment?" I shoot back suspiciously.

Jade evades the question.

"I'll bring him over in an hour," she says.

"You are not going to dump that baby with *ME*!" I thunder. "I have a book to write!"

But the line clicks and commences to burr. She's gone. I get on the phone to that vixen, Dory, faster than butter melts on a hot ear of corn.

"What appointment?" I yell.

She must have been expecting my call. That pussy-footing, double-crossing hoyden has her answer all ready. I can almost smell the perfume through the receiver.

"I have a date with my new man," she simpers.

"I *THOUGHT* SO! Well, you just call and tell him you're busy. I am not going to be the chump in this deal, no siree. I have important work to do, and you know it."

"I am not breaking this date, Sean," Dory says, so calmly it sounds like sass. "At last, I have found a man who can give me everything I need. He's been right in front of me for years waiting for me to notice him. Now that I have finally come to my senses, I'm not going to waste any time. I can't *afford* to waste time at the age of seventy-two."

"I don't care about your godforsaken love life!" I scream. "Get me out of this. She'll be here in an hour!"

"Sorry, Charlie," Dory meows. "I've got a date with

destiny. You should get one, too. It's the *ooonly* way to fly."

Enough of that claptrap. I jiggle the hook to get rid of Dory and then dial the number for my daughter, Lydia, out on Long Island. There's no answer. Typical.

Lydia refuses to install an answering machine. Says she would never ask her friends to talk to a machine. I am deprived of an opportunity to record exactly what I think of her as a parent. If she hadn't been such a blind ninny, I wouldn't be in the position I'm caught in now. She should have put that girl on the pill—or, better yet, locked her in her room until she turned eighteen. The sixties has been the ruination of us all. Lydia let those harebrained liberal ideas turn her head, and she's been a feminist ever since. A fat lot of good feminism has done for Jade.

There's no one else to call. Jade's father and mother have been divorced for years. Jade's father, Tyler, moved to Africa in 1989, when Jade was nine, to fly light aircraft for rich American men on safari. The cash he wires back every month makes it possible for Jade to have her own apartment and to support herself and Troy. Tyler is an absentee father throwing money at the girl instead of real guidance. He should be here right now to shoulder the results of his neglect. Instead, *I'm* the one left holding the bag.

I go back to work but find it impossible to concentrate. After a frustrating twenty minutes with my mind zigzagging and gibber-jabbering, I lie down to have a nap. I'll need all the rest I can get for the ordeal ahead of me. I put on my blue satin eyeshade and program my mind for lucid dreaming. I implore Morpheus, god of dreams, to help me steer my dream ship into bountiful waters. Morpheus is a Greek god, but I borrow him like this to help with my work. As long as my readers don't know about Morpheus, I can pretend to be a purist; a loyal disciple of Cagney's beloved Norse mythology.

I sink into a deep slumber; reaching theta level in a

matter of minutes. Over the years, I have trained myself to fall asleep on command and, once asleep, to dream vividly and lucidly. With brain waves oscillating at around 5 hertz, I enter my dream and begin to structure the environment I need. Cagney arrives: He's come in response to my rallying call. I sometimes convene a meeting if I don't understand where he's going with his investigations. We hash out our misunderstandings like gentlemen and hatch mutual plans for where to take the case next.

During our conferences, Cagney is a model of cooperation and professionalism. Occasionally, we call upon the gods; or we enlist the skills of the local coroner to help us with the evidence we already have. On rare occasions, we summon a witness to provide a missing link. But, usually, the two of us get down to brass tacks and resolve everything on the agenda with an old-fashioned "man-to-man."

Today, Cagney's already at the conference table going through his rituals with a fresh cigar. I am waiting for him to light it: I know he will settle into his most profound and productive thoughts once he's taken a few good puffs. I'm shuffling manuscript notes and putting pages in order when I hear a familiar voice. I look up in surprise. I didn't invite anyone but Cagney. This is definitely not part of my game plan.

It is the Norse god, Loki: god of mischief. Loki is known as the trickster god. It was Loki who engineered the death of Odin's son, Balder, by providing Balder's brother with a poisoned dart. Eventually, Loki contributed to the downfall of Odin himself. Odin was chief of the Aesir gods. When a giant wolf swallowed Odin during his last great battle, Odin's kingdom came to an end and the earth sank beneath the waves of a flood. Loki was present at that final battle; conveniently, Loki just happened to be steering the ship bearing the crew of giants that Odin was leading his warriors to fight.

Loki is notorious at stirring up trouble. He's also a master of form change—effortlessly taking on the form of a horse or falcon, or even a fly. I sometimes use Loki as a foil for the heroic god of my story; thus supplying Cagney with a devil's advocate to help thicken the plot. Loki insinuates himself into the plotline and subtly plants evidence against the wise counsel of a more wholesome god, such as Mimir or Thor.

Loki's clever imagery and manipulation of the facts seems so convincing, the reader will wind up rooting for the disastrous course of action Loki is scheming to put into play. The reader will even begin to doubt Cagney's historically astute judgment during crucial scenes. It's an effective way to increase suspense—and later, in the final scene, to once again drive the reader's admiration for Cagney to its zenith. Spencer loves it whenever I use Loki to spice up the proceedings.

Assuming that Loki must have a delectable curlicue to throw into the plot, I welcome him to the table. He leers at me and lets loose a laugh like a mighty peal of thunder. His guffaw shatters my peace of mind and blows my notes all over the meeting table. Cagney looks on, affable as ever, while cigar smoke snakes serenely around his head.

"You mere mortal!" Loki slings at me. "You blithering imbecile!" Loki crows like a dominant rooster and leaps onto the table. "You think you can control your dreams and make them fit your precious formula. Ha!"

The god of mischief is posturing upon my scattered notes while he screeches his insults at me. Surreptitiously, I attempt to ease my notes from under Loki's feet. Cagney looks on with a placid smile. Loki spots my sly attempts to recover my notes and this sends him into a frenzy of laughter. With his mouth open in titanic chuckles, he transforms himself into a lion and the laughter becomes a throaty roar.

Now he has four gargantuan paws planted squarely

on my work. His regal mane eclipses my vision. Loki is so close, I can feel his hot breath on my face.

Even though I'm utterly terrified, I can't help thinking that his eyes do look very wise. This is not the conference scene I planned to have. I try to pull myself out of the dream, but Loki uses an animal form of ESP to sense what I'm doing. He fixes me with yellow eyes; I'm mesmerized. I cannot move.

I try again to activate my powers of lucid dreaming and throw him out of my reality, but Loki is all-powerful and he doesn't budge. He transmits a thought form into my brain: It explodes first as orange light, and then gradually coalesces into simple words—words that thrum like the call of a lonely owl in the deepest, densest, darkest forest.

"Did you tell him yet, Loki, old pal?" Cagney says, like a whisper from a grave. Cagney has a raw throat from too many fine cigars; his voice gargles with congestion.

I cannot see Loki's face anymore, but I can feel his breath. The words remind me now of a wolf call in the wild; haunting and beautiful, echoing around me in a mystic fog. I'm scared out of my wits. Loki's paw nudges my cheek as I struggle to regain my sight. I am trying to blot his seductive words from my mind.

You can write anything you want to. Writing's not a nine-to-five job. Writing is like blood. Don't waste your precious blood on routine. Try something new. Don't let yourself die without exploring new realms. You can't run away from this forever—forever—forever—

Loki's final word reverberates in the mist; I shake my head violently to make it go away and tear at my eyes to escape the chains of darkness. Loki's gone, but he's pounding on tribal drums from afar. Ridiculing me. Taunting me. Pressuring me to listen.

I feel something harsh tangled in my hair—pulling me down, down, down. I wake up and realize that the strap of my eyeshade is snagged on an upholstery button embedded in the couch. The drum pounding from afar is someone hammering on my door.

"Open up, Grampa!" Jade is shouting. "I won't stop knocking until you do."

I stagger to the door and unlock the deadbolt. Jade bursts in with Troy on her hip and a quilted baby bag slung from each shoulder. She has a satin blanket over one arm, a pillow with ducks bobbing on the pillowcase clenched in her armpit, and a small Styrofoam cooler in her left hand. A collapsible playpen is propped against the doorjamb.

Setting Troy down, she deposits the baby bags and cooler on my expensive Turkish rug, flings the pillow and blanket onto my glass and rosewood coffee table, and then returns to the hallway to manhandle the playpen into my "Greenwich Village chic" living room.

With an expert flip of the wrist and foot movements worthy of a soccer champ, Jade sets up the playpen. Next, she empties the contents of one of the quilted bags onto the playpen floor. Toys, Golden Books, stuffed animals cascade in a heap like fruit from a horn of plenty. The little mother picks up the boy, gives him a loud kiss on both cheeks, and swings him over the padded rail of the playpen onto his stocking feet.

Troy stands looking at Jade for a moment and then slowly sinks. With an absent-minded smile, he squeezes a dog bone as he goes down. A faint squeak issues from the rubber bone. Troy looks as if he has just woken from a nap. What a coincidence! I feel as if the midnight train smacked me in the noggin as it rushed past en route to New Jersey. Jade pretends not to notice my befuddled condition.

"He can sleep in here tonight," she says, gesturing at the playpen. "He can't go to sleep without his blankie—that's why I brought it. His dinner is in the cooler: Make sure you slice his chicken, and the vegetables need to be heated. There's juice and fruit for his breakfast, and he can have a piece of whole wheat toast with you. But *don't* give him peanut butter. He's allergic to peanut butter."

"Wait a minute," I say, finally catching the meaning of her first sentence. . . . My thought processes are still on thirty-second delay. "He doesn't need to sleep here tonight. Just come pick him up after your ladies' meeting. I'll be up until midnight, at least, working on my book."

Jade cocks her head and stares at me as if I'm a whacko straight out of the nuthouse.

"I'm not going to drag him out of bed in the middle of the night and wake him up to get him home. I'll come and get him in the morning. By that time, I know you two'll be best friends, and you'll probably want to keep him for another day. Everyone who baby-sits him just hates to let him go. He's such a cherub."

I glance at Troy and snort. He may look like an angel but looks are deceptive. I don't trust the little blighter to be anything but a typical three-year-old. At that age, Lydia was smearing feces from her potty on the Humpty-Dumpty wallpaper and strangling innocent kittens.

"I don't *want* friends," I tell Jade with an evil glare. "You should know that by now."

"Oh, you pretend to be a monster, Grampa," Jade huffs. "But I remember when I was little, you would sneak me out of the house for an ice cream even though Gramma told you not to spoil my dinner. You bought me agates for my marble collection, and you taught me to play jacks with pigs' knucklebones. I just bet you'll be playing with Troy five minutes after I leave. You'll wish you had a sandbox in your apartment. Then you could build Matchbox car cities with Troy the way we used to in Mom's back yard on Long Island—remember?"

"This is all a fiendish plot," I say irritably, "but it's not going to work. In the movies the old man baby-sits the kid, gets all schmaltzy and sentimental, and then writes the book for the granddaughter. But this ain't Hollywood, girly, and I'm no pushover. If you don't show up by nine a.m. tomorrow, I'll take him to the day care center downstairs in the foyer and leave him with the other brats."

"Don't worry, Grampa," Jade smirks. "I'll be here by nine o'clock. And don't have *too* much fun . . . you might burst a blood vessel at your age."

She tosses her immaculately braided auburn hair and struts out the door like a mother peacock.

I slump onto the sofa and look at Troy in the playpen. He's fiddling with a buckle on his playsuit and sucking his thumb. Now that I'm alone with my thoughts again, the hideous dream comes back to me in a tidal wave breaking over my skin. I can feel a patch of sweat on my back, and my mouth tastes like a tray of month-old kitty litter.

But, I didn't learn lucid dreaming without learning mental strength. When I look at it rationally, the dream is merely symbolic of my single-minded approach to writing. Mysteries are my forte—I've made a comfortable living at this for many years. How many writers can say that? There are millions upon millions of them out there; busy writing so-called "deep and meaningful" books that will never see the light of publication. That's because these poor, deluded suckers see writing as an act of "self-expression" instead of as a business.

I started out in advertising myself: writing ads for automobiles, soap powder, and cigarettes. But after twelve years, I decided I wanted to work for myself. So, I simply developed a formula and taught myself to write mysteries. A commonsense career move, that's all.

Loki is the devil's advocate. Whatever is the wisest, most productive course of action, Loki schemes against it. He'll manufacture thought forms and frightening images to make you believe you ought to go in the opposite direction.

All the while, he's luring you into a trap.

If *Loki* is trying to convince me to write Jade's book that means I should stick to my guns and retire after one last Cagney Thoreau. Loki is a hall of mirrors. He's merely reflecting the distortion I could do to myself if I go against my better judgment. If I listen to Dory and Jade—not to mention that Crabtree buttinski!—I could end up looking like an eighteen-foot-tall fat man with eyes where my chin should be and my edges oozing like melted rubber.

The phone rings and I get up to answer it. A young telemarketing "consultant" wants to sell me a wallet full of fabulous savings vouchers for services in my local area. He is a cocky, ignorant young man and, before I let him out of my clutches, I do as much as I can to twist his mind and entice him with the mirage of a big commission. He thinks I'm going to purchase ten wallets. At the last moment, just as he's poised to jot down my address, I tell him I'm planning to report his company to the authorities "for invading my privacy and using my unlisted number for purposes of solicitation." His reaction is a delight to the ear.

After I hang up I decide to go back to work. I'm way behind schedule—this has been the worst day of my writing career. Never before has my discipline been so lax. Never before have I failed to resolve my plotting dilemmas using one of my standard tools. I average an output of 1,500 to 2,000 words per day: Today I've written 65.

As I settle into my chair at the computer, I remember to glance at the playpen. It is empty of all but toys. I scan the living room; Troy is nowhere to be seen.

In the kitchen, I still don't see Troy but I see where he's been. I like to have half a banana with my whole wheat toast every morning, so I always keep a fresh bunch in the porcelain bowl my mother used for displaying fruit when I was a boy. The bowl has been pulled to the edge of the counter—it's evident Troy managed to reach it by using the old "open-drawer-as-stepladder" trick.

I like my bananas ripe; in fact, I prefer them riddled with black spots. It seems Troy likes ripe bananas, too. He has squeezed every one of my perfectly-ripened bananas—all seven—and their slimy guts ooze from the split peels.

I contemplate Troy's fingers slathered in pureed banana and become alarmed. What is he touching at this very moment? My autographed Agatha Christie photo? My 1928 copy of *Roget's Thesaurus*? My vintage typewriter?

On my way out of the kitchen, I notice the disemboweled bag of Trojan whole wheat bread and the dish of mangled butter. My alarm grows.

"Troy?"

I try to keep my voice soothing. My true state is one of volcanic rage, but I don't want to scare him before I can get my hands on the little demon. I am too old to crawl under beds or tables in pursuit of Dennis the Menace.

I find him in the bathroom on a silent squeezing spree. The toothpaste tube sprawled on the indoor-outdoor carpet looks like the traditional 36-24-36 pin-up girl with curves and dips in all the right places. A trail of mint gel with added fluoride makes an artistic "S" on the bathmat—complete with four little toe-prints.

Troy is standing on the toilet lid and leaning across to the sink. The water is running and the front of his shirt is soaked. He's playing with a very soggy bar of Palmolive; squeezing it and rubbing nodules of soap along his arms. My medium bristle toothbrush is caked in green as is my favorite comb with the broken handle. *Macy's Hi-Styles*—the dime store brand name in raised cursive letters above the teeth—is now an abomination of green gunk.

Troy sees me and shoves his hands under the running water: a visible guilty conscience.

"Mommy no," he says, in a woebegone undertone.

"Mommy no is right," I tell him. "Mommy would be

very angry if she could see what you're up to. Does Mommy spank bad boys?"

Troy's head wags vigorously from side to side.

"Mommy *never* spank Troy. Mommy loves Troy."

"Mommy is a misguided saint," I mutter, and take Troy by the armpits to lift him down. "Saints cause more sinning than is generally advertised. Now I'll have to give you a bath. Does Mommy undress you?"

Troy's face lights up at the mention of a bath. "I can do it!" he squeals.

While I run the bathwater and test the temperature, Troy struggles to undress himself. He manages to get his red corduroy playsuit and airplane-motif undies down to his ankles but cannot get them past his Nike jogging shoes. I advise him to remove the shoes first, and he immediately gets the laces knotted beyond recall. He won't allow me to help him and gets himself into a lather of sweat trying to pull the shoes off his feet.

At last, the shoes are eliminated, and he peels off his socks. The playsuit comes off next. When Troy attempts to pull his Inspector Gadget T-shirt over his head, he gets himself entangled and confused. The shirt is covering his face: I can hear his desperation, but still he will not permit me to assist him. He sounds like an angry pony snuffling and snorting inside the shirt—tossing his head and making frantic arm movements to free himself from restraint.

Finally, I grab him and finish the job.

"Grampa NO!" he bellows, his face red. "Troy do it." He stamps his foot and gives me a look which would fell a lesser man.

"Can you climb into the bathtub by yourself?" I ask, my tone purposely thick with deference to my great-grand-son's emerging sense of self.

But Troy is already scrambling over the side. With visions of little feet slipping on the bottom and a little head cracking on the unforgiving surface, I take hold of one of his arms to steady him as he sits down. All I need today to finish me off is a trip to the emergency room with a bloody, wet, unconscious three-year-old.

Once he's in the water, Troy transforms from a boy into a threshing machine. He's giggling and splashing gallons of water over the side. Water rains down on me, and the carpet is soaked. I shout for him to stop, but Troy is making so much noise in his own private world of thrills he doesn't hear me.

At last he stops flailing and the water level settles at three inches. Now he lies back in the water with a beatific expression and "floats." He pretends to be an angel: swanning his arms slowly and crooning a holy-sounding dirge. Troy is fascinated to listen to the burble of his voice with his ears under water.

Despite my hurry-ups, Troy stays in the bath until the water's almost cold. Suddenly he feels the chill and now he's adamant about getting out of the tub. He pressures me with urgent whimpers and wild-eyed pleas for a towel.

By now, I'm cold too. My clothes cling to me and I feel unclean. I bundle Troy into a towel and carry him to the living room. Before I can place him safely on the sofa, he wriggles free and dives headfirst onto the cushions.

"Now, stay put while I get your pajamas," I tell him sternly.

But he's already off the sofa. War whooping like an Indian, he runs buck-naked and throws himself across my leather ottoman. He's on his belly with arms fanned out and legs crooked in the air behind him—jet aircraft noises swell and shudder.

"Look at me, Grampa!"

Troy tilts on his belly like an airplane banking.

Meanwhile, I'm pawing through Jade's bag of kiddy supplies. It's barely dinnertime, but already I am desperate to get Troy to bed. Finally, I locate his summer pj's at the bottom of a mountain of clothing. It looks as if Jade plans to leave this human whirlwind with me for at least a week.

Troy spots his pj's and emits a blood-curdling peal of despair. It sounds like the word "no" again—this time from a dying elk with transcendent breath control. My head is pounding and my pulse is jackhammering. I can't take much more of this.

It's as though I've stepped beyond myself. I watch myself fling the pajamas at the little boy; hear myself shout hoarsely and unintelligibly. I feel the floor shake as I stomp out of the room. Pain sears my hand as I slam the half-open bedroom door out of my path. I slouch on the edge of my bed. From somewhere above my own body, I observe my poor posture as I slump with my face cupped in both hands; breathing raggedly.

My rage drains away. The room is quiet and dark. Remotely, I feel hot tears trickle between my fingers. I cannot feel the grief which caused these tears. I'm numb.

I hear footsteps padding down the hallway. Sense a body at the door. Troy hesitates: giving his vision time to adjust to darkness. Without hearing him cross the room, suddenly two clammy hands curl around one of mine.

"Poor Grampa."

He fingers my tears. His arms move to encircle me. I'm being rocked and comforted by a three-year-old. His pajama top brushes my arm; he must have dressed himself while I was in the bedroom breaking down.

"It's OK for boys to cry," Troy half-whispers to me in his baby voice, still rocking me gently.

I realize he must be mimicking Jade. Perhaps she took a pop psychology class on parenting. Her dear mother Lydia probably taught the class—with her isocratic, radical views on gender and stereotype.

"I am just an old man, Troy," I murmur heavily in

the gloom.

Troy wisps a butterfly kiss across my cheek. I catch a whiff of something on his breath and sit up in alarm.

"What have you been eating?" I bark.

But I already know. I lurch from the bed, grab Troy by the arm, and frog-march him straight to the kitchen. Sure enough: A jar of peanut butter sits open on the floor.

"Oh my God."

I look inside the jar and attempt to judge how much he has eaten. The jar looks menacingly depleted. At least he has eaten his poison with some grace. . . . An heirloom teaspoon from the dish drainer rests against the rim of the jar.

"Troy, what does Mommy give you for allergy?" I demand in a panic as I shake him by the shoulders.

Troy answers me with his head still bobbing.

"Mommy give me crayons," he says, as if I had just suggested a cozy craft session before dinner.

The word "allergy" means nothing to him. I stare at him closely. Will his skin turn blue? Will he vomit? Just what are the symptoms of peanut butter allergy? Will he stop breathing and go into a coma?

I grab his arm and propel him in front of me to the telephone. I dial my doctor's after-hours number: A young man answers. He questions me coolly and informs me that no symptoms are in evidence. I don't trust him. He sounds like a medical student—a haughty med student from a rich family. What would he know about being responsible for the life of a child? He has probably been cocooned from responsibility for his entire Ivy League existence. He tells me to have a stiff brandy and calm down. He almost adds "old man." I can hear it longing to roll off his tongue.

I smash the earpiece back into the cradle. Troy pulls at my hand.

"Make me dinner, Grampa. Mommy put chicky."

Troy races to the cooler and pulls off the lid. He lifts

a parcel of foil from the neat pile of food and drink.

"Chicky!"

"Alright, alright."

My breathing's shallow. I feel as if I'm in the kind of crisis zone where life has an unreal quality. If Troy doesn't collapse first from peanut butter poisoning, then maybe I'll be the one to drop. Heart attack? Stroke? Perhaps I should book us both into the emergency ward for the night—just to make peace with the inevitable.

I sit down for a few moments to catch my breath. Meanwhile, Troy busies himself unpacking the cooler. He carries his field supplies to the kitchen item by item: an assortment of fruit; Tupperware containers bearing child-size vegetable portions; a purple plastic thermos of apple juice; a gaudy box of graham crackers; the foil-wrapped chicken.

By the time I reach the kitchen, Troy has the lids off Jade's Tupperware pots. He's eating cold mashed pumpkin with his cold breast of chicken. He tears bites from the slab of meat in his fist like a Neanderthal wearing leopard skins. He scoops his mouthfuls of pumpkin using the dirty spoon from the peanut butter jar. I don't try to stop him. He's in the bloom of health. Another quarter ounce of the allergen won't kill him now.

Pumpkin and peanut butter. I shudder at the taste combination. Troy kneels on a chair and eats in quiet bliss.

Troy wants a story after his dinner. I feel somewhat calmer, snuggled next to him on the sofa, reading a Golden Book aloud. The story he has chosen is *The Color Kittens*; a picture book I recall fondly from Jade's babyhood. Troy wants to hear *The Color Kittens* from cover to cover in one continuous loop. We read it together seven times: Troy's body gradually grows limp against my side. He looks sleepy and peaceful.

I pick him up and he nestles into my arms. When I lower him gently into the playpen, he doesn't protest. He curls into the fetal position while I cover him with blankie. Troy lifts his head so I can slide duckie pillow into position. I step away, and he smiles with his eyes almost closed.

"Nigh-nigh, Gwampa." His words slur sleepily.

I tiptoe to my desk in relief. The cursor blinks on the computer screen inviting me to write, but my stomach shrivels at the prospect. Cagney's a turncoat and a traitor! I refuse to finish writing this book.

In an altered state, I stare at Cagney titles on the bookshelf. I've been reduced to an antiquated zombie; my life is in shreds around my feet. My writing days are over and my health is shot. Why am I here? There's no earthly reason to go on now. No reason to live.

I sit at my desk for as long as I can. I'm bone weary, but I don't want to go to bed. I don't want to dream.

I tidy and reorganize my desk. I gather paperclips and spend time feeding them into their nifty holder: a red box with a magnetic strip around the mouth. I make a Zen meditation out of attaching paperclips to the strip ready for instant use. Once my paperclips are divinely arranged, I set to work color-grouping my pencils and pens. My mind is a blank. I care about nothing and no one in this void. What a blessing. A balm of macrocosmic surrender.

Troy stirs in his playpen. I glance at the clock: two a.m. How did so much time pass? Troy sits up and yawns. He climbs over the padded rail and comes to my chair.

"Poor Grampa."

Not this again. I don't need sympathy; just oblivion. Troy's dark hair is sweaty. It stands on end—reminding me of Jade's image of the monkey fur.

"My tummy hurts, Grampa." Troy's voice is groggy. "Hurts here."

He pats a place on the lower right side of his little abdomen . . . a spot which corresponds exactly to the sixty-year-old appendix scar on my own body. I am too tired to ignite into another raging panic, but my legs feel boneless and watery with fear.

"Let's sleep in Grampa's bed," I suggest, rising from my chair with a wobble.

Troy follows me just like a docile lamb trailing its mother. In the hallway, I have to steady myself against the wall; my legs seem ready to buckle beneath me. This is it. My time has come. I am detached as I wait for the sweet release of death. I wait, but I'm still on my feet. Troy tugs at my trouser leg, and we move on like a caravan of snails.

I'm too tired—too utterly beyond normalcy—to take off my clothes. We get into bed in the dark. My legs feel light and unencumbered . . . they could almost be floating in an ocean of warmth and relaxation. Alongside me, Troy breathes evenly. He's already asleep.

Soon I am asleep, too—fighting theta level; fighting REM. I cannot stop the dream which comes to me. Instead of entering it lucidly, I feel as if I've been shoved in the rear end by an impatient boot.

I crash-land in a blue hammock strung between two stately willow trees. I'm on the banks of a sprightly stream. Maybe this won't be so bad after all. The willows drape their curtain of green around my hammock, and I feel the way a seven-year-old boy feels in his tree house: deliciously out of sight. I can see the edge of the stream beneath the gently waving curtain but nothing beyond. I am enclosed.

I become aware of a second hammock half-hidden in the greenery. A hand parts the curtain and a face looks through. The face belongs to Bragi, Norse god of poetry. Bragi looks just like I have always imagined he would: long brown ringlets; enormous, limpid blue eyes fringed with sweeping, feminine lashes; genteel smile and soft, expressive hands.

"You're not dying, you grumpy old buzzard," Bragi remarks conversationally, relaxing in his hammock with hands behind his head. "You're exactly the kind of misery-guts who outlives the nicer folk. You'll hang on for years . . . just to make their lives a torment to the bitter end."

I'm astonished at this coarse speech. I was expecting poetry and lyricism.

"Poetry, schmoetry," Bragi bleats. He is reading my thoughts—just like Loki during my afternoon nap. "I would not waste good poetry on the likes of you."

Below us, Bragi's wife, Idunn, stretches languidly on the velvet grass. She smiles up at me like a friend. Bragi produces a bludgeon from beneath his royal blue Shakespearean cape and whacks her on the skull with it. Idunn crumbles like delicate porcelain. The dust and debris of her once comely and voluptuous body settles into the grass before my eyes.

"Why did you do that?" I cry.

"To get your attention," Bragi says complacently.

"What is it you're trying to tell me?" I beg.

Voices are swirling; floodwaters are rushing in my ears. The hammock swings violently—making me dizzy and nauseous.

Bragi leaps into the hammock with me.

"Get with the program, Gramps!" he yells, and his breath is foul. His expressive hands around my throat feel more deadly than poetic. "You're missing the boat! Last call for Paradise!"

I am struggling to loosen Bragi's grip on my throat. I wake up and find I'm choking myself with my own hands. Troy is sleeping perpendicular to my body, and his feet are gouging into my side. I'm surprised at the strength they exert: My ribs feel black and blue. By the light of dawn, his small frame is lax and his face looks cherubic.

Carefully and quietly, I inch away from his feet and ease out of bed. My clothes are crumpled and sweaty; I feel chilled by the sweat drying on my skin.

In the bathroom, I lift the lid to have my morning pee. In the bowl, ribbons of toilet paper move gently in an invisible current. Troy's unraveled the entire economy roll into the water. There is so much toilet paper in the bowl, I'm afraid to flush the toilet and risk clogging the system. I use the bristles of the toilet brush to fish out most of it and slop it into the wastepaper basket. Only then do I feel safe to pee and flush.

No doubt about it: Troy is a throwback to his grand-mother Lydia.

I take a brief shower, put on clean clothes, and wipe the crusty toothpaste from the bathroom floor. While my coffee perks, I clean up the aftermath of Troy's chicky feast and the entrails from the banana genocide.

With a fresh cup of coffee and the leftover graham crackers, I sit on the sofa and read Jade's diaries from one to twenty-six. Jade's handwriting is round and fat—riddled with flares and flourishes—simplistic and immature, even in the later volumes. She affects an old-fashioned hourglass "g" and uses a heart shape to dot her i's.

She's dead-blunt about everyone. She writes that I am stingy. Cranky. Selfish. Elsewhere, she describes how it feels to have a famous grandfather: She's proud of me and has read all of my books—even the earlier, less well-known publications such as the series starring Detective Minnow and his over-educated sidekick, Julian Quill.

When I finish reading, it's 7:30 on the dot. I check the bedroom. Miraculously, Troy is still asleep. In a fever of creativity, I dial Spencer's home number. I'm too electrified to wait until he reaches his office.

"Omigosh—Sean Dugan!" Spencer sounds giddily pleased to hear from me even at this hour. So typical of his saccharin good nature. "So, what's up in your corner of the world, my dear old friend?"

"I'm calling to break my contract," I tell him, with

no preamble. "But go ahead and sue me to the hilt. I'll be in my grave by the time you make it through the court system and try to collect damages."

I hear a tiny click. When Spencer speaks again, it sounds as if he's in an electronic tunnel.

"Well, you're the artist, Sean," Spencer says, giving in amiably. "I respect your intuition. I guess Cagney didn't have one last book in him after all."

"Cagney's a Judas," I say harshly. "He threw me to the Roman soldiers while he sat there looking inscrutable puffing that goddamn cigar of his."

Spencer makes a sympathetic noise in his throat: It bounces in the electronic tunnel like a ping-pong ball. His calmness over the bombshell I just dropped infuriates me.

"I am starting on a new book today," I announce, certain *this* news will shock him. "It belongs in a radically different genre from murder mystery. I will be ghostwriting it for someone who doesn't have the time or peace of mind to write it herself. It'll be a smash hit, and we'll go on the talk show circuit with it."

I plunge ahead with my stunning news.

"I want a new contract and a corpulent advance for this book, Spencer. If you don't give it to me, I will get it somewhere else. Every major publishing house from here to the West Coast would lunge at the opportunity to poach me from Hail Ulysses Press—and you know it."

"I certainly do, Sean," Spencer agrees. He is talking without tension as if reminiscing about the good ol' days on a Sunday stroll in the park. "What's your new book about?"

"Teenage pregnancy."

I wait for Spencer's horrified protest.

"Wow!" he says. "That *is* exciting, Sean. I can really see the potential. With your name on the cover, it will be a stellar production. I'll have Nancy get the contract drawn up this morning. Congratulations!"

Now I'm really getting suspicious.

"You're kidding. Just like that? Don't you even want to see the outline first?"

"As I said, I trust the ol' Dugan intuition." His voice brims with smiles. "You always do an outstanding job."

"You're a dufus, Spencer," I snap. "You always were a pushover, but this is ridiculous. I smell a rat."

"*Ai yi yi.*"

I catch the hushed interjection as it ricochets faintly through the tunnel. I wasn't meant to hear this—it must've slipped out in sheer exasperation—but I'd know that yappy female voice anywhere.

"*Now* I know why you seem to be speaking from beneath the English Channel," I explode. "You've got me on that damn speaker phone! Dory, what in Hades are you doing there at this hour?"

But even as I pose the question, I know the answer. Spencer's the new boy toy. God save us from Dory's libido. That woman goes through men like disposable razors!

"Oh, Sean," she scolds. "You are always so rude. Spencer is your greatest ally, and yet you drag him in the dirt like common garbage."

"He just needs to let off his steam, honey," Spencer puts in mildly. "It doesn't hurt me."

"So, it's *honey* already," I snort.

"Spencer proposed to me last night with roses and champagne," Dory gushes. "And my answer was YES."

I hear giggles and whispers in the tunnel. I can well imagine the putrid kissy-kissy transaction going on at their end of the line.

"Spare me the morbid details," I remind her. "This is a business call."

"A little sweetener in the deal never hurt anyone," Dory gurgles, sounding like she's tipsy from champagne.

Instantly, I get the real picture. Dory has paved the

way with Spencer so I can write Jade's book. He was ready to give me a new contract without turning a hair because Dory had done the groundwork. She probably didn't over-exert her feminine wiles—everyone knows that Spencer is the world's easiest sell.

When I look back on it, I realize Spencer has always been excessively attentive to Dory. Even when her opinion wasn't worth spitting on, he would encourage her to voice it and then listen in rapt attention while she spoke. I suspect he's been in love with my ex-wife all along . . . maybe even for the entire forty years of our association.

Well, now he'll find out what he's in for.

"Do tell us, Sean," Dory gloats. "What changed your mind about Jade's book? Was it the joy of babysitting our darling great-grandson? I know how irresistible he can be."

"Oh, boy," I say acidly. "The irresistible force meets the immovable object. What a mess when they collide."

Oblivious to my meaning, Spencer laughs gaily.

"Sounds as if you two had fun," he blathers.

"You must be joking," I snarl. "It was the nightmare I knew it would be. Troy came like a tornado and reduced my sanity to tatters. Smeared gooey substances on every surface and caused water damage on a major scale. Clogged my toilet, redecorated my bathroom with mint-flavored gel, and used ripe banana for the new kitchen décor."

Dory tries to cut in. I plough on; drowning her out.

"I came to the conclusion that Jade's book needs to be written when I saw how her illegitimate three-year-old could destroy my morale in two short hours. My mission is to save society from a deluge of rampaging brats. My new motto is: Teenagers should get on with being teenagers. They have no right to assume the responsibilities of parent-hood. Jade needs to tell her story, and I need to make sure it gets out there and saturates the marketplace."

Silence reigns while they digest my tirade. At that

moment, a small figure appears at my side with Rocky and Bullwinkle pajamas sagging from his bottom.

"Poor Grampa," Troy says in a clear, fluting voice which fills the quiet room. "*Ai yi yi.*"

The stunned silence on Spencer's line gives way to gales of laughter. I have the distinct feeling the laughter is at my expense.

"Oh, Sean," Dory gasps. "You're such an old fart."

She breaks into more volleys of laughter at the pungency of her own wit. Spencer's laughing just as crazily—I have never heard him sound so boisterous and brash. Dory is corrupting him already.

"I can't wait to see you on the talk shows," Spencer splutters. "I'll write it into the contract that Troy must appear with you on TV. Ratings oughta go through the roof!"

"Very funny, Spencer," I say dryly.

This conversation is getting out of hand. Turns out even Spencer is a turncoat. I get rid of them and hang up the phone. Troy is getting restless.

We eat a low-key breakfast and I let him squish the banana his mother packed for him. Nine a.m. sharp, Jade knocks on my door. Breezing in, she begins to gather Troy's belongings. Troy embraces my legs and peeks around my left knee. He watches the flurry of maternal activity with a resistant pout.

"Not so fast, young lady. We have work to do."

Jade arches one flawlessly plucked eyebrow as I tell her of my decision to ghostwrite her book. I had expected her to fly into my arms in gratitude. Instead, she assumes a bossy attitude: tells me I can write the book only so long as I convey *her* agenda and philosophies—not mine. She's just like her grandmother. Who ever put across the fool notion that females are the weaker sex? Jade's a ruthless businesswoman just waiting to happen.

But, seizing the moment amid the pandemonium of

Troy's sensory style of play, Jade and I sit down and fire off an outline. We hold a title think-tank and agree on the title, *Liberating Your Future: Informed Teenage Sexuality.*

Jade gets on the phone to Kevin Crabtree to tell him the news and to ask his opinion of our title. After she hangs up, I inform her that I refuse to be second-guessed by this anonymous Crabtree wannabe. Ghostwriter does not mean taking dictation. It means skilful storytelling—the creative delivery of someone else's truths. In other words, creative partnership; *not* lackey to every Tom, Dick, or Harry with an opinion.

"You'd better learn to get along with him," Jade advises me pertly. "Mr. Crabtree has been my mentor since I was a freshman at Cadmauris High. That won't change just because you've been hired for the job."

Mentor? Hired? This girl doesn't need a so-called mentor. She needs to learn respect. Suddenly my age, my experience, and my fame mean nothing to her! Jade is in charge, and she clearly intends to keep it that way. Now that her iron will is exposed, I wonder how Troy ended up with such a soft, empathetic nature. The little guy's a positive marshmallow compared to his mother.

When Jade and Troy go home after lunch, I sit in front of the computer and ponder the plunge I'm about to take. After forty years of writing to a formula, I'm about to venture into a totally new genre—with a non-fiction subject that relates to my life on a par with Masai warriors or space telescopes. About to enshrine my impish great-grandson as a symbol of teenage sexual awareness. About to shock my loyal fans—and toss a challenge to the bestseller's list with this radical departure from the norm. *My* norm.

I think about Cagney and my years of riding in his pocket. All those years avoiding risk and creative evolution; believing my own rhetoric about writing as a "nine-to-five job." I realize I am glad to be free of Cagney. Suddenly, he seems like just another insufferable bore who insists there is only one way.

After being trapped in my own dreamcatcher with vengeful gods—not to mention stuck in my apartment with an uninhibited small boy—I am no longer terrified of unfamiliar writing. One thing's for sure: I'd rather write in an untested genre than experience yesterday all over again.

My fingers find the keys: asdf—jkl;. I type my first sentence and it snowballs from there. By dinnertime, I've produced the first 2,500 words of *Liberating Your Future: Informed Teenage Sexuality.*

I call Jade on a high to give her the news. She responds as though I've called to tell her the weather report: deadpan. It's her payback for all those failed ploys and the expensive bribery that didn't work.

"Come on, girly," I coax. "Throw me a bone. I'm excited. This is big stuff for Grampa."

"OK, Grampa. Here are the lines you wrote in that kitten card you gave me for my twelfth birthday—the year you gave me my first diary. Remember?"

"I remember," I say, hesitantly.

What on earth did I write?

"To my darling Jade," she begins. I can tell she's reciting from memory. "A writer needs tools but most of all a writer needs dreams. Here is a tool to help launch you as a writer—now you must do the rest from your heart. Happy Birthday from Grampa Sean. Kiss, kiss, hug, kiss."

"I wrote that?" I ask faintly.

"Yes, you did, Grampa," Jade states, in a tone of reproach. "I cried when I read your card, and I loved the present. It was the best thing I got for my birthday that year. Writing in my diary helped me get to know myself better than I could have any other way. It's also been the guide I've gone to for my hardest, scariest decisions."

I feel humbled. Jade figured out the writing secret

light years ahead of me and has been using it every day to enrich her life. I, on the other hand, have almost let pride be the death of me.

But, it's never too late. I can be a seventy-two year old student and learn from what writing can teach me.

That night in bed, I drop into REM and dream randomly. No vengeful gods. No urbane detectives puffing inscrutably on cigars. When I rouse myself at 6:45 a.m., I can recall only shards of fleeting dreams; replete with symbolism but not clear in meaning.

I don't have time to analyze my dreams this morning. I need to get to my computer. Yesterday I quit my day job—today I'm just another flake writing for the fun of it.

"Poor Grampa. . . ."

Now I know why Troy kept saying that.

Smart little devil.

FERTILE MATERIAL

Zzz Judy and Henson have been married for almost one year. Judy is a late riser and a grump for the first hour after she wakes up. Henson cannot tolerate staying in bed beyond 6 a.m., and he likes to do something active as soon as he gets up. On Judy's birthday, he proudly brings her breakfast in bed—at 6:30 a.m. Describe the breakfast scene and the tiff that ensues. Use liberal doses of dialogue.

A FREAK OF TIME Browsing in the furthermost reaches of a big city museum, you become aware that you're locked in for the night. Strange noises disturb you. To your fascination and horror, a model village from another age comes to life around you. What kind of civilization do you find yourself in? Are you invisible or conspicuous to the natives? What do you think of their society? Have you brought some item from the 21st century that could alter their history—or at least create a big stir?

DUELLO* In the movie, *Duel*, Dennis Weaver is pursued by a modern-day monster: a sinister eighteen-wheeler determined to break his spirit. Get into the shadowy mind of the deranged driver, but go beyond the plot of the movie. Maybe you're the avenging wife, instead. Or the neglected son, fresh out of prison, returning fifteen years later to trace the crime in his father's footsteps.

*See Footnote #3, page 217, for notes on character copyright.

JACK'S HOUSE

Mardi opens a leather pouch and shakes a collection of oval-shaped, flat black stones onto her beach towel. Helen chooses one; delighted to find a platypus smiling underwater painted on one side. She picks up a second stone and marvels at the miniature frill-neck lizard sitting in her palm. Her third stone shows a dingo pup frolicking on the sunny shores of a Kakadu billabong.

"Where did you get these?" Helen half-shouts, above the mesmeric roaring of surf.

"They're mine," Mardi says. "I invented them."

"They're wonderful." Helen examines the remaining stones. "It must be difficult to switch from painting gigantic murals to doing animals on little rocks."

"Yeah, not my idea of a fun time." Mardi's grin is sardonic. "But there isn't much demand for murals here in good ol' Woollenghi,* so I'm branching out. Call it unabashed commercial enterprise. I'm going to sell them as sets in these nifty leather bags—like the runes you buy with a companion guidebook from the New Age stores."

"You could call them 'Goanna Stones'," Helen says thoughtfully, warming to the concept.

Mardi cocks a loaded finger at her. "Bull's-eye," she says. "I knew I could count on you to grab it by the throat. You're commissioned to write the text."

"What text?" Helen asks, in faint alarm.

---

*pronounced "woolen-guy"

"The text explaining the symbolism or the essence of each stone." Mardi replies calmly, squeezing 15+ in fat white globules along her suntanned thighs.

"But I don't know anything about it!" Helen protests.

"You're a writer," Mardi says. "Do some research and then wing it. That's what writers are for." She massages the blobs of lotion into her skin with long, slow strokes.

"I can't screw around with this sacred stuff," Helen tries to insist. "A tribal Aboriginal would be better for the job. This is highly ancestral to Aborigines. Thirty thousand years worth of myth and legend is nothing to get commercial with."

"Oh, rubbish!" Mardi retorts. "The last time I was in Melbourne, I met an Aborigine who played the didgeridoo in the showroom of his Dreamtime art gallery. There I was, feeling the vibration in the pit of my stomach and wondering if I was about to channel wisdom from Old Man Kangaroo, when his cell phone rang in the middle of the performance! He was selling the traditional dot paintings from his childhood desert tribe for thousands of dollars and limited edition CDs of his didgeridoo recordings. He was computer savvy, too. You can't afford to be a purist in this day and age, baby. Just write the text. You will have copyright exclusivity, and when these little mothers hit the market you'll be raking in half the royalties. See? You've got nothing to lose!"

"OK," Helen says absently, sifting sand through her fingers. "I'll give it a go."

Mardi rolls her eyes. "Don't knock me over with your enthusiasm, girl!"

Helen sighs and shades her eyes to look out to sea. She feels too depressed to try for a saucy comeback.

"The trouble with you, Hell-on-Wheels," Mardi says, giving her shoulder a playful push, "is this: You've got no self-belief. Ya gotta get some fire in your belly, woman. Drop the tentative crap and take it by the scruff. Show 'em what you're made of. Use bluff, if necessary, but get out there and do it!"

"I can't," Helen moans. "I just can't. I've developed a terminal case of writer's block."

"The Dingo Creek manuscript?" Mardi grills her.

"It's unraveling at the seams," Helen says. "I've been flowing with this novel for three months: brainstorming the storyline and caressing every subtle lead. It has literally been giving birth to itself. Then, suddenly—bang. Everything went flat. Now the characters are just going through the motions in a dreary plastic landscape."

"Hmm." Mardi jiggles a Goanna Stone as she muses on a possible fix. Her face lights up. "Maybe what you need to do is ditch that dead puppy and start on something fresh."

Helen grimaces to herself. This is precisely the advice she always dreads.

"I *know* I ought to be professional about it, but I'm so attached to this story I don't want to let it go." Mardi's deep in contemplation as Helen talks. "When I think about abandoning it to begin something new, I feel as if—"

Mardi drives her fist into the towel.

"I'VE GOT IT!" Up on her knees, she does a rock 'n' roll dance in self-delight. "What you need is a new *setting*. It gets the juices pumping for me every time. Whenever I can't seem to crack a painting from one angle, I travel around my subject one hundred and eighty degrees and paint it from the other side. That way, it's a whole new landscape."

Mardi looks so smitten with her own brilliance, Helen decides to play along just to shut her up.

"You're right. . . . What I need is a classic setting like Paris or Rome," she acquiesces. "Anyone could write inspired stuff set in Italy—especially along that gorgeous coastline."

"No, no, *no!*" Mardi shrieks. "Don't be such a moron, Hell-on. You don't have to get on an airplane or use an encyclopedia to beef up your setting. The best writers know how to use any turf—even their home turf—to their own advantage."

"Woollenghi," Helen murmurs. "Population: 3,000."

"Woollenghi is just fine!" Mardi overrides her. "If you can't seem to capture that atmospheric tone because it feels too humdrum or too 'close to home' then change the name to something that looks Australian but starts with a different letter—or maybe alter the syllables to give it a whole new flavor. But, it sounds as if *you* also need a new taste sensation with your hometown. You've obviously been viewing Woollenghi from a jaded perspective."

Helen nods. She is still staring out to sea in a bottomless gray mood.

"You're right . . . I do feel jaded. I feel as if the sleepy town of Woollenghi is the perfect match for Helen Bayliss the writer—uninspired and commonplace. No one wants to read another boring book set in Dullsville, Australia."

"Argh!" Mardi emotes, burying her face in her hands like a character from a tragic opera. "You need some serious occupational therapy, honey child."

* * *

Two mornings later, Helen is agonizing over the fire scene in Chapter Eight when the telephone rings. It's Mardi; voice pregnant with triumph.

"Go, baby! We've found the perfect Gothic setting for your novel."

Helen flinches at the word "we."

"Hacienda San Frijo . . . five kilometers out of town on the banks of a balmy waterhole. Which isn't exactly the running water of your working title—but you can always use artistic license to transform it into that babbling brook of yours known as Dingo Creek. We happen to be lucky because Tony knows the owner, Jack Lemuel. Good ol' Tone's gonna meet us out there tomorrow morning to introduce us to Jack, nine a.m. sharp. I'll pick you up."

Helen's heart sinks at the mention of this intimidating

and unpleasantly provocative name. Tony Jespersen: a friend of Mardi's from her university days back in Melbourne. Helen knows only too well that Tony is a poet, a musician, and a gifted glassblower whose work sells briskly in the tourist traps and galleries along the Mid-North Coast.

In addition to his talented studio work, Tony is in demand as a performer. He reads his poetry at a local wine bar once a month and is also the good-looking drummer for the local band, *Wongala Man*. Tall and bronzed, with the blond unruly mane of a surfer and the genteel speech of an educated aesthete, Tony is a man for all seasons.

On the two brief occasions she was exposed to him, Helen did not know what to say. To her, Tony Jespersen's the quintessential unblocked artist—forever creating, performing, or collecting payment for his art.

Helen wonders whether Mardi has told Tony how this expedition to Hacienda San Frijo is supposed to be the cure-all for Helen's latest humiliating case of writer's block. Given Mardi's average level of restraint, Helen knows the odds of keeping her affliction a secret from the scintillating and flawless Tony Jespersen are probably close to zero.

After Mardi's phone call, Helen loses all ability to concentrate on the intricacies of Chapter Eight. She takes out her journal and tries to freehand some inspiration.

> *Hacienda San Frijo: the setting for passion, betrayal, and genesis among the inhabitants of Dingo Creek. But what is an Aussie house doing with a Californian-style name? That'll have to change for sure!*
> *[Study assignment: look up Aboriginal place names, Crystal Harbour Public Library.]*
> *And just who is the mysterious Jack Lemuel? Is he character material himself? Or perhaps a mentor; a patron of the arts.*

Helen feels an intense desire to impress this paragon, Jack Lemuel. Ashamed at the egocentricity of her desire, she tries to isolate and eradicate it from her emotions.

> *Jack will have a penetrating gaze; will sense things about a person without being told. He will be well-traveled, sophisticated, slightly aloof. A foreigner by birth, he's been ignited with a volatile love for the untamed, primordial essence of Australia.*

She ponders for a moment with her pen poised: What age bracket might this cultured immigrant belong in?

> *Jack is a man in his middle forties; classically minded and widely read—perhaps with an artistic streak of his own. He will naturally ask me what my novel is about. Oh dear God, how I dread that question! My responses are always so limp.*
>
> *To add yet more curry to the stewpot of degradation, Tony Jespersen will be there to hear my less than spectacular reply. That she-devil Mardi has a lot to answer for.*
>
> *When Jack pops the question, maybe I could look enigmatic and murmur, "I never discuss my first drafts with anyone but my agent." Jack doesn't need to know that the pompous and reverend agent-on-high, Ms. Victoria Smythe-Fleming, never so much as returns my phone calls let alone takes me to lunch on her expense account.*
>
> *I'll have to warn Mardi to keep her ambassadorial instincts in check. Must tell*

her not to encourage questions from Jack.
I'm supposed to interview him. I should be in
charge; the one asking the questions.

But in her mind, Helen feels Jack Lemuel taking on the glow
of superhuman mystique. One word of encouragement from
Jack, and she knows she can shatter the mightiest monolith
of writer's block that life could ever hurtle in her path. Likewise, one syllable of scorn or indifference from the lips of her
new mentor is primed to devastate her beyond recall.

When Jack Lemuel looks me in the eye, he'll
either recognize my vocation or he'll recog-
nize a fake.

Like a sinister disease-carrying microbe, she shuts her journal
and isolates it in a drawer. The tumor of self-doubt inside of
her is already more than she can bear. Any reminder of the
challenges of Chapter Eight instantly brings on lassitude and
dread.

The following morning, her manuscript shimmers in
the sunlight like a beckoning mirage. Helen looks at her desk
with misgivings. Her adored copy of *Macquarie Thesaurus*—
hanging together with its last threads of binder's glue—pins
down a handsome disarray of chapter notes. Her delectable
copy of *Making Stories: How Ten Australian Novels Were
Written* coos from a pigeonhole above her keyboard. Every
cherished tool of her craft bristles with invitation from the
shelves or calls to her from piles on the floor around her desk.

Helen visualizes herself screaming with the convul-
sion of crippled artistic muscles too traumatized by failure to
uncurl. In the typical yin and yang of their friendship, Mardi
chooses this moment to make her breezy entrance.

"Looks as if I should be taking you to the Woollenghi

Regional Hospital for Tortured Writers," Mardi observes with a wicked smile. "Preferably the emergency room—pronto."

"Shut up, Mardi," Helen hisses. She despises her best friend with an upsurge of maddened grief in her throat. "You don't know what it's like."

"Ha!" Mardi spits like an asp. "Every damn artist and writer on this planet knows what it's 'like.' I have been to the catacombs of hell and back with every blank canvas or rendered wall I've ever put my trembling brush to. I just hope when I'm in the clutches of it myself, I'm not sanctimonious like you are when you're singing the writers' blues. What a martyred schmuck! God save us from your pampered sensibilities. 'Poor l'il me. I'm the only one who knows how it feels. I'm the only one who's ever suffered this way!' Get a *grip*."

Helen is wordless with humiliation, but her eyes are fireballs of rage. Mardi deflects these fearsome emanations with a satisfied smirk.

"At least you're angry today," she comments. "Makes a nice change from mopy and depressed. Well, I'm not sitting around here like a shag on a rock. Let's go."

Helen shoves a notebook and pencil into her bag and tries to compose her disjointed emotions. Snug in Mardi's sporty little hatchback, they head out of town and drive north for a kilometer to the junction at Fernleigh Creek. At the intersection, they turn off the highway onto Tallowwood Road. In less than a mile, they've traded the cultivated sameness of Delgado's commercial strawberry plantation for the relative wilds of outer Woollenghi.

Houses out here are scattered: Rural properties and hobby farms on the western side of the road coexist with the ragged bushline. Gum leaves glint silvery olive in the sunlight. Beyond a tranquil grazier's homestead, in a low-lying mist, a robust Mallee bull with a venerable cowlick on his forehead benignly crops the dew-soaked grass.

Helen wonders wistfully why she has never thought to

explore this road herself. She is still pissed off at Mardi, so she keeps her thoughts, feelings, and deepening grudge resolutely shrouded in silence.

At a point where Tallowwood Road breaches a gentle hill, Mardi pulls into a rutted driveway. She churns through a muddy patch of open ground leading to a soggy, uncut lawn of mint and kikuyu grass.

They come to a stop next to a mud-splashed, weather-beaten Land Rover: Helen nervously identifies it as Tony's weekend runaround. Her seething mental checklist of Mardi's faults gives way to stage fright. She doesn't even have time to rehearse something intelligent to say—Mardi's already out of the car, laughing and yakking with her tall and gorgeously suntanned college friend.

"Hello, Helen," Tony says, shaking her hand loosely in what Helen interprets as bored condescension.

Helen smiles tremulously but does not speak. She is wishing this ordeal was already over and she was home crying therapeutically in her bed.

As a threesome, they stroll across the lawn toward the house. Inwardly, Helen rechannels her attention to the task at hand and begins the addictive process of observation. She flips open her notebook and commences to jot.

The first dynamic that moves her about Hacienda San Frijo is the sprawling incongruity of its layout and design.

> *What a higgledy-piggledy fairytale creation.*
> *Is this the mind of a bohemian at play? Or the*
> *work of three or four capricious architects*
> *pasted together?*

Tony and Mardi stop to wait for her. Helen is transfixed by the wrought iron symbol dominating a stone feature wall. On a clean page of her notebook, she draws a capital *P* with a lower case *x* through the downstroke.

Esoteric . . . yet somehow familiar,

she scribbles, and then hurries to join the others. There is so much to investigate and catalogue and yet she's still only outside in the yard.

Conning tower lookout; U-shaped house creates a courtyard; claypipe tiles on crazy roof,

she adds in haste as Tony knocks discreetly on the door.

Norfolk pines; rough-hewn fences. Jumbled Spanish romanticism fused with the homely lines of frontier ruggedness.

When the door opens, Helen's fantasy of a refined, erudite mentor for her writing career is shattered. Jack Lemuel is eighty-two years old; stooped and sun-dried; his abundant chestnut hair interfused with handsome veins of silver. Something about the suspicious brown eyes and brush-cut moustache reminds Helen of European fortitude. As Jack motions them inside, his voice issues formidably from the ramparts of an imperious breastbone.

"This way, this way," he chides, ignoring Tony's gracious introductions. "This is the present-day living room—"

So begins the tour of Jack's house—with no personal acknowledgements or preamble whatsoever.

Soaring stone fireplace,

Helen notes, feeling a dismal tide of dispossession.

Celestial stained glass doors.

The onrush of creative euphoria Helen had felt in the court-yard only serves to heighten her newly disenchanted life. Jack proudly smoothes a velvet fold of the stately garnet drapery suspended from oversized curtain rings.

"This room's the core of the original building," he continues, his eyes glassy with far-off memories. "It functioned as the first butcher shop in town. That was long ago: back when the market promenade of Woollenghi was located out here in the hills—complete with B.G. Pullen's one-man sugarmill and Mrs. Vietko's mouse-infested general store."

Helen takes notes on Jack's spiel as fast as she can jot. Jack pulls aside a velvet curtain to reveal a sumptuous double bed on a raised section of parquet floor. The parquet, thickly treated with polish, still manages to looks mellow and honey-drenched with age.

"I use this as a guestroom now." He blinks fast and rocks unsteadily on his heels. "But in the olden days, this was the killing block for our purebred cattle. We hand-raised 'em, slaughtered 'em, and hung 'em up for sale. . . . Made all the deliveries meself by horse and cart—"

Jack's torso is racked as an ancient-sounding cough robs the oxygen from his lungs.

"—or on horseback in really bad weather." He goes on without missing a beat in his monologue. "All that started back in 1933: the year I blew into town with naught but me pocketknife and a yen to settle down. After twenty years of thriving local trade, I up and bought meself a new FJ Holden panel van—and, by golly-gosh, didn't that newfangled breed of horsepower make those old deliveries a piece of piss!"

Laughter explodes from him and degenerates quickly into a semi-desperate wheeze. But Jack shuffles across the room as though life is getting past him in the outside lane and he's on the chase to run it down. As the members of Jack's new captive audience trail him into the hallway, Helen's pencil pushes madly across the page.

J.L. doesn't detect nuances or decipher souls,

she scrambles, not bothering to stay between the lines.

> *J.L. much too busy reliving old times to no-*
> *tice the slightest thing about us. Not sure he'd*
> *know what a "novel" was even if it bit him on*
> *the behind. But J. could write the unofficial*
> *history book on W. He was an eyewitness—a*
> *local mover & shaker in this town.*

Jack lingers near the staircase. He is regaling Tony with epic tales of building materials and shipping costs made cheap by overland bullock drives. Helen grabs this downtime to study the Spartan theme, but sumptuous length, of the hallway.

"Look at this," Mardi whispers from behind. "Is this divine, or what?"

An extensive part of the eastern wall is dominated by an enormous sliding barn door; freshly sanded and varnished to retain its functional but elegant lines. Helen shivers at the gory origin of another Jack the Decorator masterpiece.

> *Again the slaughterhouse architecture. Brass*
> *cowbell hung above sliding barn door. The*
> *bell's leather strap, painted gaily with yellow*
> *and red blossoms, conjures a cowherd's sim-*
> *ple existence in the freedom of the Alps.*
>
> > *Whitewashed walls; raw slate floor;*
> > *light, breezy atmosphere. Well, no wonder:*
> > *The hallway is unbuttoned to the sky at one*
> > *end! Any passerby could vault the waist-high*
> > *mudbrick wall and land inside the hallway*
> > *uninvited.*
> >
> > > *Potted African violets line the top of*

the barrier . . . as if to welcome intruders
with the niceties of flowers.

Mardi is mulling over the same bizarre, open-air feature.

"Whadd'ya plan to do with this unfinished section?" she badgers Jack, during a rare break in his diatribe.

Jack looks at her without appearing to comprehend who it is. The identity of audience members is not important.

"Ah, you mean my 'trust window'," he beams. "The view is priceless."

He points over the mudbrick wall to a paddock being grazed by a small herd of cattle. Jack's spirit swells, almost visibly, to some exalted private domain.

"But—but—thieves could jump the wall any time and help themselves to whatever they can grab," Mardi exclaims in disbelief. "Or even murder you while you sleep!"

Jack waves it off. "Oh, I am well-protected." His tone implies spiritual privilege and predestination.

Behind the old man's back, Tony wags a finger at the girls with a roguish, knowing expression.

"He'll never listen!" His lips move in silent, exaggerated speech. Not that Jack would notice even if it *was* aloud.

Tony's gaze lingers on Helen for a moment: Helen is glaring at her notepad; sighing in disgust. The interview questions she'd sweated over and rehearsed have been left for dust by the unasked-for tour of Jack's bizarre house—his number one pride and joy and the only topic of discussion permitted.

Jack and Tony climb the stairs with a bemused Mardi dawdling in their wake. Mardi is still mystified by the "trust window." Helen watches as Mardi stops on the midway landing at a well-used saddle lying astride the crude-cut ironwood rail. She throws one leg across the saddle.

"Yipee-*yee*-ha!" Mardi hollers, pretending to buck like a cowgirl in a rodeo. Helen can almost see the cowgirl's chaps.

Helen's grudge from the "poor me" scene is beginning

to thaw. She follows Mardi up the stairs while trying hard not to break into a grin.

The L-shaped staircase takes them around the corner from Mardi's saddle and upward another uncarpeted flight into the abbreviated second floor of Jack's house. This is the hacienda's own lookout—a Spanish-style turret—the crowning glory of the rowdy, ramshackle roofline which had piqued Helen's interest from the ground. She can't wait to see what manner of refurbished novelties Jack might be hoarding upstairs in his loft.

As they reach the upper landing, the stylish—if somewhat motley—décor shifts accent from its clean sense of rustic refinement to one of sheer neglect and fifties-era bad taste. The upper landing is an insipid shade of heat-blistered, flaking pea soup.

Even the beautiful inlaid timber lintels have been ruined with horrible green paint,

Helen mourns in her notebook.

Large transom windows inset the walls on three sides . . . but at a preposterous height. You'd need a ladder to see the view. What a stately country lookout this could have been given a little commonsense.

The window glass above our heads is filmy; the cobwebs encrusted with grime. The ceiling peaks high above half-rotten raw timber crossbeams. Noisy crimson rosellas have wedged their nests in the uppermost shadows of the house. They dart and swoop—"kweek-kweeking" over our heads like bombers in the Pacific intent on defending their turf.

"This way, Helen." Tony is at her elbow steering her into a tiny room. "This is Jack's bedroom—full of untouched history. Sixty years' worth, in fact."

Helen surveys the mess. Jack's bedroom is thinly paneled with naked chipboard which emits a low thwopping tone as it shudders in the currents from the hallway draught. Beneath their feet, rutted floorboards creak and groan at every footstep or slight change of stance. In one corner, a narrow camp bed sags in the middle; made up roughly with rumpled threadbare sheets and a solitary camp blanket.

A low-set, unscreened window facing western ranges is thrown open to the cowpie-scented breeze.

"Jackie-boy must freeze to death up here at night," Mardi mutters, in unconcealed distaste.

"Probably not, you know," Tony corrects her in a low voice. "Jack Lemuel has pioneering blood. This guy runs on a tolerance for pain and discomfort which puts our cushy lifestyles to shame."

Gouged & lacerated teak table; frayed wicker armchair with no cushion,

Helen is busy writing as they whisper.

Antique dresser has water-damaged mirror: a mildewed reflection of our shapes. Dresser top awash with debris of J.L.'s life. Old can of talc; rusty tobacco tins; bird shit on his 1955 copy of The Graziers' Almanac.

Silver currycomb—teeth caught with clumps of horsehair. . . . Is this the source of the musk of animal that lingers in the room? Jack's bridle and bit ensnarled with a length of frazzled rope; sorely corroded pulley wheel

knotted on at one end.
Age-old stratums of dust suffuse Jack's
bedroom with denied loneliness.

On the table sits a leather bound, water-spotted copy of *Lives of Saints*. The book lies open at a reproduction of Raphael's Vatican masterpiece: *Saint Peter's Release From Prison*.

Noticing Helen's avid curiosity, Tony shakes his head.

"Don't even ask," his lips move again in soundless discouragement. "You'll only set him off."

Helen is irritated. Tony seems to fancy himself an expert on the subject of Jack Lemuel.

Jack is deep in conversation with Mardi; pontificating fondly about the sweeping view from his bedroom window.

"If you know where to look along the skyline," he tells her, his dogmatic speech heavy with nostalgia, "you'll spot the old fire rangers' tower up on Knobby's Lookout."

Mardi stands in the breeze from the cow paddock and squints in the direction his trembling forefinger points.

"Used to deliver a carcass of me best to the rangers up there before they shut down the rangers' tower and let it go to ruin. Had to splash the creek at Gallagher's Crossing and take the scenic crescent through to Bark Hut Road. Helluva steep climb up Bark Hut on horseback with a side o' beef on board; I can tell you that much for sure." Jack chuckles ruefully.

Tony bends to rescue a battered acoustic guitar from the shadows beneath the camp bed. As he picks out notes and tunes the strings, Mardi's rapacious, hazel-flecked green eyes sift through the chaos of dusty books, mementos, yellowed newspapers, and horse-riding tackle. Black and white photos with the old-fashioned serrated borders speak of an odyssey spanning three continents . . . a youthful generation gagged in stifling tradition but with an itch to break old ties.

Jack turns and notes what Mardi's zeroed in on.

"Born into this mortal life a Swiss Jew," he proclaims,

as Mardi draws breath to ask. "These snapshots of the Old Country are the only remnants of the old Jack. At fifteen, I blasted outta there, like shot from a cannon, bound for the splendid shores of the U.S. of A. Had meself a devotional singing career in San Francisco, California before you could say diddly-squat."

Jack preens his chin in profound thought.

"Family didn't know what hit 'em. One minute I was slaving in me father's foundry for a pittance; the next minute I was on a steamship to New York City. Worked hard below deck for my passage. Landed belly up in New York and then took off for the West Coast the very next morning; doing odd jobs for me bread and board along the way."

Helen takes feverish notes while Tony strums softly in the background. Jack, intoxicated with his own history, shows no signs of coming back to earth.

"San Francisco: Brother Anselm of The Holy Church of the Impoverished found me starvin' in the streets. Took me in and put me in the choir so I could earn my daily keep. Told me to set my sights on heaven and train my vocal cords to follow suit. Yours truly obeyed his instructions to the letter and practiced for hours every day—nearly scared myself silly with the power of me own voice. The power of *faith*!"

Jack is drugged and besotted but Mardi finds a way to break the spell. She plucks a photo from the litter of memories on the table.

"Who're these old bazookas?"

Jack cranes his neck to have a look. From her position on Jack's left, Helen makes out three elderly, rotund women sitting on the foredeck of some kind of European paddleboat. All three are imprinted with the same dour expression.

Stern Swedes appear to be subjecting themselves to a river cruise. . . . Helen frames the observation but doesn't get as far as transcribing it into her notebook: She's too shocked and embarrassed by Mardi's rudeness.

The hefty female enthroned in the center of the sour, staunch little group is wearing a dashing, tightly-curled green mustachio. The mocking yet undeniably jaunty soupstrainer has been applied in ink directly to the surface of the photo.

Why, oh, why did Mardi have to home in on this one?

"Those are my sisters," Jack replies resentfully, after a long, uncomfortable silence.

Helen is positive she's going to shrivel to nothing and die of the side effects of shame. Out of the corner of her eye, she catches Tony's shoulders heaving. Helen suspects silent laughter, but Tony's face is bent low over the guitar and she can't see his mouth. She feels indignant at his lack of respect.

"Why is this sister wearing a mo?" Mardi demands, tapping a finger on the imposing figure of the middle sister.

Helen itches to feed her stubborn friend through a wringer and then peg her out to dry.

But, far from being insulted, Jack's hacking laughter erupts from the mucus in his lungs like a popcorn maker popping gravel. He laughs so long and so violently, he has to bend over and put his hands on his knees while he recovers from the coughing spasm which follows.

"Bossy-boots Margrethe, the oldest sibling," he gasps finally, "has worn the pants in our family from the day me blinkin' father passed away in '49. So I slipped the witch some facial hair to befit her proper station in life. Me father had one just like it."

Jack, using his cuff to wipe a tear from his eye, shows his thickly tartared teeth in a death mask grin.

"Anyone who cheats her baby brother out of his share of the family inheritance deserves no less," Jack adds, with a righteous sniff.

Helen is stunned.

J's heart putrid with ancient family poison.
Where is the forgiveness?

She carries over to a fresh page and puts down key words from the scene she has just witnessed. Her plan is to flesh it out later at home.

By now, Mardi has really hit her stride. She goes on to prod Jack about a faded, but official-looking document she has teased from another pile of junk. A fancy gold letterhead trumpets the heady announcement from the Bilpingan 20th Annual Architectural Convention, Bilpinga, 1956.

"These guys give you some kind of smart-ass award?" Mardi wants to know.

"Oh, them." Jack shrugs. "BAAC was going to honor me for my 'unique building style' and the preservation of an historic site. But—surprise, surprise—the award got bogged in their fuddy-duddy code of ethics.

"So sorry, Mr. Lemuel," he mimics in a plummy tone. *"We simply cannot bestow a Certificate of Excellence upon a building with no existing blueprint. You have added an extra two wings and an upper storey to the original dwelling with no documentation whatsoever. We must do justice to posterity. We must carry on the tradition of public safety. There is simply no shire clerk's filing of your alterations."*

Jack rolls his eyes as if to indicate "I could care less."

J.L. not hungry for temporal glory,

Helen jots.

> *Or is it just his mulish streak? J.L. likes to be in control . . . loves to assert his opinion as the gospel truth.*

She is vaguely aware of Tony setting down the guitar behind her. Her thoughts are honed in on Jack and his self-righteous, pigheaded stand against the world.

The prompt she needs to connect her to something crucial is niggling at the edges of her mind. Helen loses track of the others in the room for a beat of infinity as senses a gift from her subconscious.

With a noiseless footfall and a subdued clearing of his throat, Tony materializes at her side.

"Getting everything you need?" he inquires now, with tender chivalry. Tony looks over her shoulder at the skeleton scenes and dialogue scrawled across the page.

Helen draws back visibly and flips her notebook shut. She is conscious of how badly her timing's off—knows her withdrawal looks like a histrionic stunt; as if playacting a fit of the sulks—but she can't help herself.

The bland and well-mannered interruption of her exquisite inner process makes her want to expunge Tony from all privilege of contact with her creative methods . . . whether or not he cares. The mere notion of Tony Jespersen looking at another page of her notes makes her feel violated. Her connection with that elusive strand of inspiration has snapped like a brittle heartstring after trauma.

"Whatever value I did get just died a pointless death," she blurts, in a savage undertone.

Tony's lip curls in an ugly, knee-jerk response.

"Y'know, Ms. Bayliss, your attitude kinda sucks," he fires back, and then walks off to the landing to join Mardi and Jack. The protagonists are locked in debate over land tax and property values and oblivious to all else.

Helen thunders silently with shock. Every nerve in her being feels impacted by the act of counter-rejection from the once-revered Tony "Wongala Man" Jespersen. Her mind shrieks with self-denunciation. Her feet make robotic moves to catch up with the others now walking single file back down the stairs. To add to the clamor, an explosion of Mardi insults from a recent fallout with her best friend mushrooms like a radioactive cloud inside her brain.

"You're such a goddamned drama queen, Helen! You always have to 'feeeel' everything as if it's your one and only day on earth. Why don't you just get blotto on red wine and write something brilliant in a drunken fog? D'you think the drongos who buy bestsellers are gonna appreciate your stupid finesse? Get real, babe. Readers just want a cheap thrill—not your rancid artistic Puritanism."

At the foot of the stairs, Helen comes upon Tony making his hasty and overcompensated goodbyes.

"I'm running late for a commissioned work," he says, glancing pointedly at his watch. "My filthy-rich client wants to be there in person to witness the birth of her very own glass menagerie."

Reasserting his failed masculinity in front of a blushing Helen, Tony shakes hands heartily with Jack. "See you at the billiards comp on Friday night, mate. Round Twelve—our big chance to make a thrust into the winner's circle together."

"My oath!" Jack agrees, pumping Tony's hand with animated vigor. "We'll butcher 'em in their boots, me boy."

Tony grins like a war comrade. "I'll let myself out," he winks. "You finish giving these girls the tour."

Extracting his right hand from Jack's robust, double-handed grip, he hurries for the door.

Mardi looks at Helen.

"What's wrong with *him*? Spurned our poor Tony and his studly advances up in the garret did we, m'dear? Trust you to act like Miss Priss just when things finally get interesting."

"I assure you, that was the last thing on our minds," Helen snaps, but Mardi doesn't hear her. Jack is holding forth yet again.

"This is the Empress Room where my boarders lived."

He's showing them a bedroom almost the same as his own—except that this one uses twice the floor space as the room upstairs. But, the same neglected mess; the same powdering of dust. The bed is a walnut four-poster sporting the tattered remnants of a once-stylish silk mosquito tent. A graying feather comforter with almost no plumpness remaining in the panels lies on the mattress like a forgotten rag.

"Why don't you fix this room and sleep down here?" Mardi pesters. "This has the makings of a classy bedroom."

"Give me fresh air and a view of the hills anytime," Jack snorts. "It's like trying to breathe in a bloomin' air raid shelter down here—all boxed in like a Christmas fruitcake."

Mardi's incredulous. "How *can* it be when half a *wall* is missing from the hallway out there?" she says. "Just leave the bedroom door ajar and you've got the best ventilation in town!"

Appearing deaf to Mardi's challenge, Jack wanders off down the hallway. He opens a door at the end of the passageway and they follow him into the strange and rudimentary kitchen. Helen flips her notebook to a new page.

> *The walls in the "kitchen" are glossy red with the trim a horrid shade of glossy lime. The original wood stove's still intact—looks a century old at least and caked in rust.*
>
> *Where does J. cook? No electric stove; no fridge or freezer in sight. And no windows either. The counters are full of sawdust.*
>
> *An old ice safe squats near the screen door. . . . Did an iceman once deliver blocks of ice to keep J's meat and milk fresh?*
>
> *Why is this room painted in the colors of a super-hero comic book?*

Mardi stares intently at a focal point above the kitchen table. In black paint applied to the red wall, employing ornate and biblical hand-lettering, the message "For we walk in faith" delivers a solemn reminder of chastity in the garish room.

Jack barely breaks his stride as he leads them through

the kitchen. While Mardi and Helen linger, trying to satisfy their curiosity, he stands humming impatiently on the threshold of another room—a room he seems inordinately keen to usher them into. Finally, Mardi elbows Helen and they hasten to where Jack waits; tapping a foot and harrumphing through his mustache like a circus ringmaster.

Jack bows in the doorway. "Now for the best part."

As they enter the third and final wing of Hacienda San Frijo, the context of the house shifts markedly. Here is a light and airy, spacious room with an overtly public function: an entire wing given over to a formal meeting place. The room is large with superior amenities and clean, modern surfaces.

Helen and Mardi are mystified. At the head of the room is a speaker's platform where a wooden lectern holds an open book. Helen feels certain it's a copy of the bible.

The walls are an eggshell hue. Banks of windows set in the flanking walls of the room allow for plenty of sunlight and a play of breezes—giving this part of Jack's house an uplifting aura of freedom and good cheer. The wooden floor is swept and polished to a gleam. Row upon row of picnic chairs with armrests and flowered seat pillows await good company and the music of happy voices.

At the rear of the meeting area, Helen inspects the impressive kitchen arrangements.

Shiny new fridge; matching gas stove; even a microwave oven. Gigantic hot water urn for coffee and tea; double sink with stainless steel draining ramps. Cupboards and cutlery drawers filled with sturdy plain china, milk jugs, and fluted teaspoons for the tea service. Trays with lace doilies and dainty porcelain sugar bowls. Gaily colored dish towels conjure up a bustle of community-minded spinsters, aunties, and grandmothers dishing up

slices of home-baked apple pie or pavlova—
or perhaps layered sponge cake replete with
raspberry jam and whipped cream filling—
while gossiping gently over steaming cups of
Bushell's tea.

The bathrooms are equally well-equipped and clean—one for the Ladies and one for the Gents—with a storeroom full of mops and brooms and detergents in between.

"What *is* this place?" Mardi beseeches. "Some kind of reception hall for weddings?"

"We do have weddings here now and then," Jack says calmly. "This is a church."

"A church?" Helen and Mardi chime together.

"A house of worship," Jack confirms proudly. "No denominations; no ties to the Vatican. It doesn't even have an official name. Just a humble place for folks who want to get reacquainted with the Lord."

Helen and Mardi stare at one another in alarm while Jack ambles serenely to the lectern. At last, he can give them their heaven-sent treat.

"I'm gonna kill Tony Jespersen for this," Mardi vows, through clenched teeth.

Jack riffles pages self-importantly. Suddenly, as if he's found the specific antidote for their sins, he slaps a page. He clears his throat officiously and begins to read.

"Then Peter went up to him and spoke: 'Lord, if my brother wrongs me, how often must I forgive him? As often as seven times?'" Jack looks up for emphasis. "Jesus answered: 'Not seven, I tell you, but seventy-seven times.'"

"If his dear sister's green mustache is anything to go by, Jack's draggin' the low twenties," Mardi murmurs.

"Matthew 18:21-22," Jack informs them piously and shuffles the pages again. "Ah, yes," he mutters finally, raising one palm in a command for respect. "Letter to the Hebrews."

He pauses . . . appears to be communing with some profound thought process or sanctified inner voice. Then, all at once, he rings forth with a mighty bellow:

"A WARNING!"

Helen's nerves implode and Mardi lets out a screech.

"LET US NOT ABUSE THE GREAT SACRIFICE!"

Jack's eyes turn toward the ceiling in reverence and awe. The remainder of the passage erupts like a volcano from the underground recesses of his memory. His voice engulfs the room—reverberates for an agony of endless minutes—until he hits a pinnacle in tempo and volume. His eyebrows lock horns as he sacrifices his victims to the blessed inferno.

"How much more dreadful a punishment will he be thought to deserve who has poured scorn on the Son of God, treated like *dirt* the blood of the agreement which had once made him holy, and insulted the very Spirit of grace? For we all know the one who said: 'VENGEANCE BELONGETH UNTO ME, I WILL RECOMPENSE.'"

Dropping his voice dramatically, he throws a whisper from the podium which sends a shudder down Mardi's spinal column and moves Helen to squeeze her eyes shut in dread.

"Truly it is a terrible thing for a man who has done this to fall into the hands of the living God!"

Jack steps back from the lectern and wipes his brow.

All three of them are wrung out and in desperate need of fresh air. Jack wears a glazed look as he leads them to the public entrance of the church.

They step outside onto dewy grass into the incredible vista of the rolling valley. Sunlight bounces off a nearby pond and sparkles at the tips of wavelets whipped up by the morning breeze.

"Never should've let the beggars talk me into it!" Jack bursts out, gesturing at the sweetly rippling water. "Damned shire council blokes kept at me until I gave in. Said I'd be 'doing the community a priceless service' and blah blah blah.

Right here on my land, they'd found the prime spot for a dam to increase Woollenghi's water reserves—or so they believed back in 1954. They swore the engineers had done their home-work. Now the flamin' thing's defunct and they've gone and built a new one out beyond Five Gum Bluff. . . . All the latest technology and rah rah rah. As for me, those wily surveyors got away with a helluva lot more footage than they disclosed in their leaky contract! So now I'm stuck with this man-made piss pot right on the doorstep of me church."

"But it's such a pretty little lake," Helen protests. "You wouldn't ever guess it was man-made."

"Hmph."

Jack stalks off and turns a corner out of sight. Mardi and Helen pick their way through shin-deep grass snagging sharp and thorny "farmer's friends" in every crease of their clothing.

"We'll never get all these off," Mardi groans. "They stick like the devil himself."

When they manage to catch up to Jack, he's waiting in the open courtyard formed by the three unmatched wings of Hacienda San Frijo. The courtyard is still in full shade, and the grass here is the same soggy, uncut lawn they had crossed earlier to knock on Jack's front door.

The aroma of mint crushed by their feet as they walk gives Helen a heady feeling of sensuality mixed with pangs of regret. She's still feeling ravaged by the scene with Tony in the Spanish turret. She wishes she could cleanse it from her heart like unwanted blood.

Jack goes to a corner of the courtyard where a hand-made wooden ladder is nailed to the wall. The rungs provide just enough gap for a narrow toehold. Jack starts up the lad-der like a monkey up a tree and Mardi does the same.

Helen tucks her notebook and pencil into the waist-band of her jeans and gingerly takes the first rung. Halfway up, she hears Mardi calling her name.

"Hoy, Helen! Haul your britches up here ASAP, girl. This is dynamite!"

When Helen reaches the top of the ladder, she finds herself on a flattened section of the roof which runs along behind the lookout and Jack's bedroom. The makeshift deck is sizeable, and Jack has civilized it with an ironwood handrail; the twin of the rail mounted on the staircase inside. The view is spectacular.

They are looking across the back of Jack's property eastward toward Woollenghi Beach and the Pacific Ocean. The ocean is blocked from sight by a forest of eucalyptus on the eastern side of the highway. The abandoned town water supply nestles in a bowl between the lush, poorly fenced paddocks. The fields are pleasantly dotted with Jack's hobby herd of cattle. They feed amid a smattering of scribbly gums spared by pioneers when the land was cleared for grazing.

To the north, Wedding Bells Forest stretches into the faintly smoky horizon. Beneath them, the stockyard—a sun-bleached ghost of its once useful self—is a maze of sagging, decrepit corrals; spotted with dead black lichen and swamped in waist-high weeds.

By far the most breathtaking element of the beauty laid out before them is the towering grandeur of the Moreton Bay fig. The tree stands near the chimney corner of Jack's house. Huge, irregular branches allow the sunshine to filter through and dapple the ground below. The unbelievable span of foliage manifests as a powerful feat of nature—a paragon of symmetry and gravitational defiance.

From the base of the tree, the trunk rises and divides itself into a dozen massive arms. The outermost branches reach in vertical directions to lengths that seem to rewrite the laws of physics. Helen and Mardi stand gazing in transcendent ardor while a warm and gentle wind fondly tousles the leaves. The wisdom and strength of the tree permeates their bodies and realigns their souls.

If Jack holds a storehouse of history on this amazing feature, he is busy keeping it to himself.

The sun is hot and the tarpaper soon becomes sticky beneath their shoes. Jack motions for them to follow his lead again. Helen's dreading the downward climb so she's relieved when Jack crosses the deck, lifts a burlap bag hanging from the outside of the turret, and disappears inside. When Helen and Mardi do the same, they find themselves full circle on the upper landing outside Jack's bedroom door.

"Pickle me possums!" Mardi blusters. "Why didn't we come this way in the first place?"

Jack, looking unfathomable, does his crab-like hobble toward the stairwell. Helen wonders how the heck he manages to move so swiftly with such a stiffened, senile gait. They trail him downstairs into the hallway only to find he is leading them into the courtyard once again—this time, by way of the sliding barn door.

The three of them wade through the mint and kikuyu grass and round the corner at the opposite wing so Jack can show off his second pride and joy: the barn itself.

Helen's near-overwhelmed writer's aesthetic is stirred afresh by what she sees. She retrieves the notebook from her waistband and attempts to capture the spirit of heritage that the barn implies.

> *Elegant double doors; each panel twice the height of a six-foot man. Inlaid with slants of graying timber streaked black with age—like the pattern on Jack's parquet floor. We enter by pulling on the gigantic beaten-steel rings sunk into ponderous slabs of Tasmanian oak. A funnel of sunlight rides the disturbed air, and the interior of the barn is stormy with whirling motes of dust.*

"This is our special dance floor for the church meetings." Jack caresses it with his grubby shoe. "Seasoned jarrah wood laid in a single day by a team of parishioners on a summer working bee. We christened our new floor with non-alcoholic rosé and a square dance that very Sunday."

Mardi and Helen admire the superlative handiwork while an exuberant Jack throws his arms wide and begins to sing in baritone.

"You can't get to heaven from a *dance* floor—"

The low, booming registers of Jack's voice echo in the empty barn. He does an expert soft-shoe shuffle with his eyes half closed.

The whimsical moment—along with the second line of Jack's song—are obliterated by the rumble of an approaching machine. Helen and Mardi watch from the threshold of the barn as a well-polished Harley-Davidson, complete with faux diamond-studded upholstery and burgundy fuel tank, roars into the yard splattering mud in thirty directions.

The hair on Helen's forearms prickle as a burly man in black chaps and muscular leather jacket dismounts, pulls off his black helmet with the silver Viking wings, and tosses a strawberry blond ponytail over one padded shoulder.

"Warren!" Jack shouts. "It's the prodigal son himself!"

The biker lumbers at them; helmet under one arm.

"I'm not *his* son, mind you," Warren grins.

He's addressing Mardi and Helen who stand together gaping and speechless. Jack grips Warren's Herculean gloved hand and shakes it athletically as if he, too, is a hulking enormity of youth and maleness.

"Jack means the *story* of the prodigal son—from the bible," Warren adds, conscious of their baffled faces.

Jack nods. "Luke 15:11-24."

"I've come for some prayer, old man," Warren says to Jack, clapping the old man on the shoulder. "I'm starved for a decent worship, mate. Haven't had meself a decent worship in over a fortnight. Except by myself before sleep—which is never as good as feeling the Spirit move in the bosom of your very own church."

Jack looks pleased at being validated. He looks as if he wants to gobble Warren, Mardi, and Helen for dessert with a pitcher of clotted cream.

"Your timing's inspired, my son," he says, in a fervid unleashing of passion. "We're ready to bring on the Spirit."

Mardi makes a fuss of gaping at her watch.

"Helen! Have you seen the *time*? We're supposed to be in Jandiru in less than an hour!"

"Oh, yes. . . . Of course," Helen backs her up lamely. "We really must make tracks."

"Wait," Jack cries. "I have something for you."

He races off toward the house leaving them standing with Warren—who alone seems comfortable with the ensuing silence. Helen fidgets with her pencil and even Mardi looks noticeably ruffled.

"C'mon, c'mon," Mardi says, under her breath.

Helen can't help her compulsion to study Warren in secret. She makes some quick mental notes on Warren's appearance; reminding herself to write it down later at home to add to her Hacienda San Frijo stockpile.

Muddy jackboots and torn black T-shirt under half-zipped leather jacket; three-tone tattoo of writhing dragon peeks out from rip in shirt. Silver cross dangles from skull & crossbones stud in one ear lobe. Four consecutive knuckles on left hand carry tattooed message in blue: H-A-T-E. Other hand spells out the other polarity: L-O-V-E.

Warren crouches to sit on his heels and contemplate.

"Jack taught me to memorize this plain truth," he says slowly. "I am the vine and my Father's the vine-dresser. Every branch in me that bears no fruit He cuts away; while every branch that does bear fruit He prunes—making it bear even more fruit."

Warren smiles at them; free of guile or sophistication. Helen feels compassion welling in her throat. Nevertheless, she's relieved and grateful when Jack shows up with a stack of post cards in one hand.

"You can have 'em," he tells Helen, shoving them at her with an uncharacteristically direct gaze. "They're the last of the print run."

The post card is a glossy, professional photograph of Jack's house shot through the staggered branches of a row of Norfolk pine. The yellow border along the base of the card reads "Hacienda San Frijo" in medieval-style stemmed calligraphy. Beneath it, in a sober, homespun font, is proclaimed: "For every house is builded by some man, but he that built all things is God. – Hebrews 3:4."

Helen assumes Jack is bequeathing the post cards to the one he recognizes as the writer of the pair. She is amazed that Jack even took in such a detail—given his total obsession with his own little world and his oblivion to the individuality of the people around him.

Mardi and Helen say goodbye to Warren. Diplomatically, they thank Jack for the tour of Hacienda San Frijo. They can both tell that Jack's thoughts are already plugged into the sacred mission before him: He barely seems to notice their departure.

In the car, Mardi drives Helen home without uttering a word. Neither of them have the mental energy right now to analyze their perceptions aloud. They know they can always compare notes on Jack and his eccentric house on the phone or over coffee in town.

At home, Helen is restless and feels herself churning with unresolved needs. She gets rid of her shoes and socks, changes into her favorite pair of comfy shorts, and heads for "back beach" on the south side of Woollenghi headland—the beach the tourists don't know about.

As she walks barefoot along the tide line, she ponders

the events of the morning. She is still smarting over the exchange with Tony, but Helen knows there's something deeper eroding her ability to assimilate and transmute.

She tries hard to dredge up that intangible link—the clue she'd sensed within her reach up in the Spanish turret—but success eludes her.

OK, she thinks, taking a tougher line with herself. Go back to Chapter Eight. It's gotta be in there somewhere, dodo-head. Just do the arithmetic. Convert the formula.

Mentally, Helen reconstructs the fire scene. This time the house on fire is Hacienda San Frijo—but with a suitably antipodean name instead of the Spanish-Californian one Jack used from his days in Brother Anselm's care. Something like "Ambawonga" or "Tullabungwa." . . . But Helen knows the name is not worth a nit-pick session right now. No point in having a name if the entire concept doesn't work, she reminds herself glumly.

At least her two chief characters, Roger and Kinsey, snuggle into this imposed environment like peanuts in a shell. She's confident she can rewrite the entire manuscript based on the new setting. That isn't the problem.

The problem is: The fire scene has no guts. It reeks of a device brought in to spice up a stalled plot. Like a predictable episode in a soap opera, it feels too contrived to gel with the integrity of the rest of the story.

Helen realizes even the "cat on the burning rooftop" sub-scene needs some extra oomph. Cleo's safety is of heart-wrenching concern to Roger and Kinsey—that angle is solid enough. But there has to be something more. . . .

Helen knows the answer to that one is also solid. All she needs to do is to coax it from the nether world of her subconscious. She is 99% positive something crucial signaled to her only seconds before Tony's "good manners" destroyed her concentration.

After two hours of pacing and kicking up salt water,

Helen feels her ability to reshape the fire scene has gone from hopeful to snap-frozen to fossilized. With a benumbed heart, she realizes Mardi is right: She'd be better off dropping this book to embark on a new story. It's just too stressful and demoralizing to carry on this way, she thinks in despair.

Helen trudges home and slumps onto the living room couch; head resting in dejection on her favorite throw pillow. Sleep comes rapidly: the unhealthy sleep of a stun-gun attack interlaced with graphic and disturbing dreams.

She naps this way for hours . . . until the phone ringing on the coffee table across the room drags her back into a doped state of semi-consciousness. She lies in angry apathy and waits for the answering machine to kick in.

"This is Helen Bayliss at 451-9717. Leave a message after the tone."

Three computerized beeps sound and then a familiar male voice comes on the line.

"Helen, it's Tony. Are you there? Please pick up."

She stays put.

"Helen?"

Silence on the machine and then the blessed dial tone. She sinks back into the chaotic world of her dreams.

Helen isn't sure how much later it is when she hears a knock at the front door. As she struggles to open her eyes, she feels disoriented and besieged by the intruder. It's dark outside . . . why isn't she in her bed? When she realizes she's on the living room couch, she groans. The last time she napped on this couch it resulted in six costly visits to the chiropractor.

She stumbles to the coffee table, activates the touch lamp, and then blinks her way to the door in a foul mood. It's Tony; standing in the shadows of her unlit verandah.

"I know I was a jerk today," he says, peering at her through the screen. "Just give me one chance to apologize."

Sullenly, Helen unlocks the screen door for him. Her eyes feel like sockets stuffed with greasy, grainy cotton wool.

"When I said your attitude really sucks it came out all wrong," Tony entreats her, blundering over the threshold into the lamplight. "My pride was hurt by your rejection and I was lashing back. But, listen. . . . I've read both your novels and I was very moved. Mardi told me you were nominated for the Victor Katchel Literary Emblem in 1995. You really shouldn't torture yourself this way. Mardi reckons you're a shipwrecked genius, and I agree. If only you could stop your self-sabotage, Helen, you might actually enjoy writing—instead of living in this self-made limbo."

She feels as if she's hearing a blurb about a luminary in a magazine. It's all too risky to think it might be true. She doesn't want to splinter into a million shards of defeat all over again—trying to fulfill the illusion of a "successful" writer.

Turning her back, Helen paces the room. She stands by the geranium on the windowsill and fiddles with a velvety leaf. How soon will he go and leave her to her well-earned depression? She can't wait to close the door behind him and go back to sleep. Tony follows her with his newfound zeal; seemingly hell-bent on rubbing her nose in the wasteland of her potential.

"You know, there's more to Jack's house than a great setting," he says, standing behind her at the window. "I know how appalled you were by Jack, but he poured his individuality into that house. It's that fiery spirit of his that keeps him so nimble at the ripe old age of eighty-two."

"Oh my dear *God!*" Helen yells. She spins around and shakes him by the arms. "Jack is the fire chief. He spots fires from Knobby's Lookout and then rides his horse to town to sound the alarm. He drives his men—the men of the Dingo Creek Volunteer Fire Brigade—with bible quotes and prayer. He whips up their courage with his bull-roaring baritone. He strikes the fear of God into them with the imagery of sin—sin as interpreted by Jack from reading *Lives of Saints*."

Tony looks bewildered.

"And Warren . . . *Warren* is the one who risks his life to climb that stupid ladder and rescue Cleo from the burning roof. The big-hearted biker and the crabby saint. The perfect foils. What I need now is a fictional name for Jack."

Helen hurries to her desk and pulls herself up to the keyboard. In a moment, she has her word processor program up on the screen and she's digging through the Manila folders on her desk looking for her original outline of Chapter Eight. Sand from her feet and ankles scatters onto the carpet as she rolls her desk chair aside to open a drawer. Helen plucks the notes from a hanging file and sets to work.

She tries out a few invented names on a piece of scrap paper—Jake LeMarr, Jonas Yakov, Jerrod Helprin—and feels the fireworks of free association launching in her head.

She decides on the name Jake LeMarr. With this new tool in hand, she scrolls to the frustrating and stale fire scene near the bottom of page 156 where the former nonentity of a fire chief arrives to organize his men.

Helen reads several paragraphs from the screen and then uses a red pen to add fresh fodder to her outline notes.

> *Roger and Kinsey frantic about the Moreton Bay fig. They're worried the bull-headed fire chief has overlooked the tree's safety. Roger confronts Jake LeMarr: reminds him the tree is at the corner of the house. If the flames leap across to its branches, the death of the fig tree would be an unforgivable tragedy.*
>
> *Home owners' insurance covers damages and a house can always be rebuilt. But a living testament to divinity like this tree cannot ever be rebuilt or reimbursed.*
>
> *The tyrannical fire chief will brook no interference. Jake and Roger battle it out—in full view of a time bomb of smoke and flames.*

Tony stands by her desk; unsure of his role. . . . Is he a first-time guest waiting for permission to make himself at home? Maybe he's the Invisible Man. Helen works as if she's alone in the house. She is behaving like a novelist in the throes of an all-nighter.

Tony bends, unlaces his shoes, and pulls them off.

"I guess I'll make some coffee," he remarks, to no one in particular. "This could be a marathon."

FERTILE MATERIAL

SPACE CADET You are an alien named Gwörk. Your solo spacecraft ran out of gas, so you were forced to land invisibly in the parking lot of the local SkummiMart. While wandering lost in this strange, strange land, you find an abandoned camcorder. You remember how to use this prehistoric implement! For the next 24 hours, you film the curious dimension known as Planet Earth.

JEKYLL & JEKYLLER You are a sweet and kindhearted kindergarten teacher. On any ordinary day, you're a beautiful woman with refined, exquisite taste. Your secret weakness is chocolate-coated raisins. The problem? This innocent snack alters the chemical composition of your blood. Every time you eat chocolate-coated raisins you morph into a cruel parody of yourself. Describe yourself on a normal day—and then on a day when you simply cannot resist your favorite snack.

AMBER IS FOR CAUTION You are one of the traffic lights at a busy intersection. Are you red, green, or amber? Perhaps you're the left turn arrow. Describe what you see around you and how the traffic behaves. Describe your relationship with the other lights. You are fed up with being controlled by a dumb computer, and you're certain you could do a better job when left to make your own decisions. What happens when you rebel and break out of the computer programming?

THE WAY DEMPSEY WORKS

Stephanie walks into Ranchos Coffee Co. and checks behind the Moorish heritage door propped open to catch the breeze. Her favorite table's unoccupied. She sets down her laptop and leather satchel and goes to the counter. Bridget is working the morning shift.

Bridget knows Stephanie's regular order off by heart: latté and biscotti. Stephanie chooses her biscotti from the big jar—a decadent chocolate model studded with almonds and glazed with dark chocolate along the bottom. Bridget makes small talk while she steams the milk for Stephanie's latté.

"Will you be writing today?"

"Yes, I am working on my book." Stephanie blushes. Questions about her writing make her nervous.

"I notice you come in every Friday to write," Bridget says. "Does your boss give you Fridays off?"

Stephanie grins and looks pleased. "I work for myself. I'm the boss who gives me the day off."

"Wow, that's great!" Bridget yells, over the roar of the espresso machine. "I envy you. What do you do?"

"Business consultant," Stephanie replies. "Not exactly earthshaking stuff in a small town like this. But I can set my own hours—which is great for a hobby like writing."

"Oh . . . I see." Bridget sounds surprised. "It's only a *hobby*. You don't care about being published?"

Stephanie groans. "That's the two million dollar question, Bridget. You don't even want to *hear* all the baggage that comes with it!"

Another customer comes to the counter and Bridget goes into multi-task mode: ringing up Stephanie's sale while she levers open the door of the mini-fridge with one foot. Stephanie carries her coffee and biscotti back to her special table and begins her Friday ritual.

First, she moves the small lamp from the center of the table to a wide, low-set windowsill which overlooks the tables outside on the porch. The windowsill is cluttered with poetry books, potted ivy, sage sticks, and delicate New Mexican clay pieces, so this is not a simple task. After rearranging the window décor without success, she relocates two stacks of poetry books to the conversation corner behind her table. This frees up enough space for the lamp to sit next to the ivy.

The "conversation corner" is an ankle-high platform piled with hippie-style pillows and art journals published regionally in Albuquerque, Santa Fe, and Taos. Stephanie hopes the corner will not be used today—at least not by any pairs or groups. She knows her concentration is easily fractured when people are chattering and laughing only a few feet from her workspace.

The table is now ready to accommodate her laptop. She opens the lid and boots into the operating software. By now, her latté has cooled enough for the first cautious sip. She dunks her biscotti and it comes up dripping foam. Seductively, she sucks the foam and part of the chocolate away from the still-firm core of the biscotti. Her tongue is burnt by the mushy, coffee-drenched biscuit. Stephanie loves the crunch of almonds in the middle of every hot and soggy bite.

Next, she drags a Southwestern-style wooden bench from the sofa to her table. She props her satchel on the bench so everything will be within reach.

Being "organized" doesn't help ward off the clammy palms and thicket of goose bumps crawling at the nape of her neck. She wipes her palms on the legs of her denim overalls and finishes off her biscotti with one swallow.

Her satchel is bulging with tools of the trade: Pens; legal pads of lined yellow paper; a ring-back notebook from Wal-Mart for daily writing practice . . . music cassettes and a portable tape player with headphones . . . a printout of her manuscript . . . articles torn from magazines; a well-thumbed *Roget's Thesaurus*; a pint-size reference handbook. Things she loves to surround herself with to put her in the mood. She extracts the thesaurus from a side pocket and places it within easy reach.

The satchel has four deep pockets and a zipper for the center storage panel. The giant bronze zipper will not quite zip past the trio of how-to books wedged in the center pouch. *Wild Mind* by Natalie Goldberg. *The Right to Write* by Julia Cameron. John Steinbeck's *Journal of a Novel*—the intimate chronicle of Steinbeck's work habits for the manuscript *East of Eden* in a format of daily letters to his friend and editor, Pascal Covici.

Stephanie pulls out all three. She reads one chapter from each while savoring the second half of her latté.

She's dreading the next step in the ritual. It's tempting to simply continue reading—a clever front for pretending she's doing "important research" on being a writer. Whom does she need to fool by having a front? She knows the short answer: herself.

The fear is erupting in the depths of her belly: inflaming her cheeks; constricting her throat. Stephanie fiddles with her pen and reminds herself that wanting to be a writer and actually *doing* the writing is like the light and dark sides of the moon. The writing being the dark side . . . the unresolved side. The side she wants to run away from.

She pushes the laptop to the far side of the table. With a sinking feeling of fatalism, she opens her ringed notebook and marks the date in the left margin of the first fresh page.

Her writing practice notebook is about thirty per cent full.

Stephanie resists the urge to go back and read some of her previous entries; knowing this would only be throwing a panacea to her emptiness—like eating a favorite comfort food. Compulsively doing a word count on a piece of her own writing is another bad habit she's been trying to break. A word count lets her know she has a "body of work" going on. While she counts, she imagines an editor or a literary agent nodding sagely—approving of her level of output.

Stephanie realizes this kind of projection is not good for her health. She realizes she is obsessive from lack of self-esteem. She recalls that Natalie Goldberg once wrote: "We need to let writing be writing and let it give us what it gives us in the moment."

Which means WITH NO STRINGS ATTACHED, she tells herself. No expectations of having it published. No candy floss fantasies of impressing all those faceless reviewers.

But Natalie's been writing for over twenty years! She's a seasoned published author. Her books sell in the USA and England . . . they sell in New Zealand and Australia; even South Africa.

It's different for Natalie, Stephanie wants to howl at the moon. Natalie has the magic. She lives like a writer. She writes about writing in Parisian cafés. She doesn't just steal one day a week to agonize over a lone novel manuscript.

Natalie's a force to be reckoned with. She has already made her mark in the world. She can afford to write for the sheer luxury of it. Natalie doesn't have anything to prove.

Stephanie takes a deep breath; tries to calm her mind. *Mental self-sabotage is not productive.* She states this in her heart with a clear and silent resolve. Putting her pen to the paper, she disciplines herself to fill the first line with words.

>   *I bought this notebook for the sole purpose of doing writing practice every day.*

What a dreary old sentence, she thinks. What a monumental waste of time to even start. She is trying to follow that little rule she has read so many times in books for writers—to write what she knows. But her "writer's lament" seems to be all that she knows. Her belabored analysis of why she can't just take off and soar.

> *It was heady, energizing stuff buying a new notebook to devote solely to writing practice. It was exciting. It was delicious. The range of potential flashed before me: I couldn't wait to dive in and get started.*
>
> *The reality of actually opening this notebook to begin felt like a big anti-climax. My impulse was to cover the first page with something divine. I wanted my opening sentence to shimmer—to be something mystical. A truth or an insight. Instead, it was this: "I glance at the clock, see that it's almost 10:30 a.m., and wonder whether a day spent writing will matter one iota in the grand scheme of things."*

The radio station Bridget's tuned to this morning is beyond aggravating. Stephanie would like to ring the DJ's neck. His corny patter about Y2K is strident and overplayed, and he just won't quit. Between songs, he keeps it up. His plummy studio voice and tragi-comic sound effects are crowding her reality. If he doesn't stop soon she's going to lose it. She feels a primal scream coming on.

Stephanie puts a Native American drumming tape in the player and sets it to rewind. The headphones are sound-proof, and they engulf most of her head. She feels like Mickey Mouse whenever she wears them. Her dad's an old-fashioned ham radio buff: He has dozens of pairs just like these.

She uses one of her dad's adapters to plug in the jack. From experience, she knows these headphones will make her scalp ache after prolonged use. At times like this, it seems to be her only recourse. She needs privacy and peace to get her creative juices flowing—but within the right public setting.

Whenever she gripes about the rampant distractions of Ranchos Coffee Co. to her best friend, Annalise snorts and rolls her eyes.

"Then write at home where it's quiet, ding-a-ling!"

But Stephanie knows she needs the cachet of writing in a coffeehouse to fire up her motivation. And . . . something about putting herself on the spot in the company of others. A "higher power" to be accountable to (if only her fellow coffee drinkers).

But even the love/hate stimulus of her setting doesn't help much when she's down to the wire. Like the stupid writing practice she's working on this morning. She can feel the sludge she's creating with every word. Her sentences ferment together on the page like rotting flesh in a Louisiana swamp. The flesh of her own banality. Her arthritic, crotchety, corpse-like prose.

Cocooned within the privacy of the headphones and the visceral world of native drums, Stephanie forces herself to continue.

> *I wish I could launch into flights of fantasy here in my notebook. The point is to keep my pen moving—to write as a form of action. It's a way to get writing experience—to loosen up and not censor what I put on the page.*
>
> *But it seems redundant to go on and on like this! If I'm really loosening up, where is all that wild inspiration? Where's the leap from navel-gazing "stream of consciousness" into my imagination?*

> *Last night, driving home from Santa*
> *Fe, inspiration <u>was</u> happening. An onslaught*
> *of story ideas, vivid imagery, snatches of dia-*
> *logue. Badly wished I had the micro-cassette*
> *in the car with me so all those ideas wouldn't*
> *just vanish into the mist!*
> *After forty-five miles, I had a dismal*
> *feeling those ideas would no longer be special*
> *by morning. The act of receiving ideas was*
> *an adrenalin rush. . . . The energy of free-fall*
> *imagination was irresistible. But, as soon as I*
> *visualized committing my story ideas to pa-*
> *per, they all seemed pointless and over-rated.*
> *Nothing but a tired rehash of postured scenes*
> *inside my head.*

The further Stephanie takes this old familiar theme the more
ashamed she is of her own self-absorption.

> *I knew I would not be able to recapture that*
> *initial innocent starburst—that divine stroke*
> *of spontaneity. By the next morning the ideas*
> *would reveal their true nature. Unoriginal—*
> *boring—insipid. I've already lost the plot on*
> *where it was supposed to take me. . . .*

Stephanie warps back to the present dimension and realizes
she is frowning excessively. She hopes no one is watching her.
A frowning woman wearing jumbo headphones, chewing the
dry skin on her lip, scribbling furiously in a notebook: Not an
attractive look by anyone's standards.

She notices a man sitting at the chessboard table. He
has moved the chessmen to make more room for his writing
pads—the same yellow legals that Stephanie carries in her old

satchel. The man is bent over his work.

Stephanie is accustomed to seeing writers in Ranchos Coffee Co. Most of them work alone; although, every Friday a group of women writers gathers to read their work out loud. The readings are interspersed with timed writing practice à la Natalie Goldberg.

Stephanie has considered joining them but is afraid it will be a detour from her true course. She's afraid her double Sagittarius, extrovert tendencies will give her a false sense of belonging. She goes back to her notebook.

> *Ironic how I can be outgoing in "real" life but such a chicken when it's only on paper. What is so scary about writing things down?*
>
> *Now, let me try to recall those story fragments from last night . . . see if I can reproduce that electronic state where the wires were touching inside my head.*
>
> *Even as I write that sentence, my ego tries to defeat me. My mind tells me the ideas are already "way beyond stale."*
>
> *"Give up the charade. Don't quit your day job. Your ideas suck. Go get a life. Treat yourself to a pedicure and stop aspiring to be something you're not."*
>
> *My mind can say anything it wants and still get off scot-free. But, if I so much as have the DESIRE to write down a harmless idea, I get mentally crucified for it.*

This is ridiculous, she thinks. I'm gonna switch to the laptop.

According to Stephanie's private standards, the laptop is for "serious" writing. The Wal-Mart notebook's just a warm up for the real work.

Pulling the laptop into position on the table, she goes

into the C:\ drive, scrolls down the icon tree to "Writing," and opens a folder labeled "Story Ideas." She clicks on a file called "Idea_Template" and uses Save As to create a new file called "Driving_Brainstorm."

The flurry of activity is over. She stares at the screen in mild panic.

Stephanie designed her "idea template" as a crucible. The template demands refinement of an idea in such a way that specifics cannot be avoided.

Phase I is for character development. Phase I features a section for the physical description of the main characters asking for hair and eye color, height, weight, and complexion. Also clothing style, shoe size, birthmarks, posture. Shape of nose and eyebrows. Even appearance of the teeth.

The section on personality asks for food preferences, star sign, favorite authors, I.Q. level, secret fantasies, sense of humor, and Hollywood idols . . . childhood traumas, attitude to friendship, style of handwriting, sleeping habits, choice of keynote color for the bedroom setting . . . level of strength in the face of adversity, emotional response to illness or death of loved ones, inhibitions or otherwise re talking on the phone. The A-Z of main character likes and dislikes.

Phase I includes sections for lifestyle, career, marital status, parenthood, and finances. A name box requires everything including middle and maiden names. The age profile specifies time and date of birth along with the character's age during the period(s) dealt with in the story.

Phase II is where the narrative unfolds. The template provides Stephanie with questions designed to elicit a beginning, a rough story line, and a workable ending. Space is provided for dialogue samples and the charting of chronological events. A proposed twist in the plot is material for Phase II; along with flashbacks, setting, and point of view.

If an idea cannot survive this rigorous development, Stephanie discards it.

Annalise wonders why Stephanie can't "let the story happen"—can't let it tumble out from the "wild child" within. Stephanie claims that the crucible method produces a deeper story, because it demands specifics.

"Everyone knows specifics are what strong writing is made of," Stephanie tells her primly.

Annalise says she thinks the whole thing sounds anal-retentive. Stephanie tells her to go eat donuts and leave craft to the craftsman. Annalise says Stephanie reminds her more of a control freak than a craftsman.

Stephanie rebels against the voice of Annalise in her head. She's determined to put her ideas through the crucible. She gets up and walks to the counter to order another latté.

Bridget is making beverages for three people at once. While she runs the espresso machine, Stephanie has ample time to study her surroundings.

The man at the chessboard table has brought his own coffee cup. The name "Smith" is visible on the side of the cup in blue collegiate lettering. She wonders if this is his name. She knows he fills his cup with Columbian Roast from the air pot. She had seen him get up for a refill while she was busy creating her Driving_Brainstorm Word document.

He looks absorbed in his writing. His pen is the same black and gray PaperMate Flexgrip Ultra Stephanie favors. He's hunched over his legal pad and his hand moves rapidly across the paper. He does not look "relaxed" or "fulfilled" or "imbued with the beauty of self-expression," but he does look authoritative and self-reliant. Stephanie is impressed.

She returns to the laptop and faces up to the idea template. Blowing gently on her espresso, she ponders her brainstorm experience from the night before. As she rakes through the ideas in her mind, she can clearly see that all but one of the ideas are designed more for nebulous writing sessions in the notebook—rather than a structured story format.

Now that the duds have been eliminated, she puts the

remaining idea in the crucible to test it for integrity.

In a text box at the top of the template labeled "Two Minute Summary," she writes an outline; attempting not to peg her expectations too high or censor the flow.

Cezanne is 32 years old, and she creates a new world for herself each month. She wants to experience what it feels like to be a belly dancer. A French wine taster, an English aristocrat, a Scandinavian forest dweller. An Egyptian housewife in the 19th century. An Indian fakir, a Kentucky jockey, a Roman priest. She makes no judgments from within these personas: She wants the osmosis to be unbiased and true.

Cezanne immerses herself in the food, the culture, the customs, and the dress. Her research is done via books, movies, language cassettes, and documentaries.

She learns a smattering of the native tongue. Dons the costume. She feels, thinks, and behaves in the ethnic role of the month; decorating her workspace to reflect whatever culture she's bringing to life.

Cezanne earns her living by running a stall at the local flea market. She features Spanish heritage jewelry, incense, medicine bags, Tibetan singing bowls, Polynesian artifacts—anything exotic, traditional, imported, or symbolic she can get her hands on.

Acquaintances view her as eccentric. Her friends are used to her quest for understanding, and they lap up the diversity as it washes into their own lives through Cezanne. They look forward to the monthly ethnic din-

ner parties, and they're usually curious about whatever Cezanne is learning. She provides them with a distilled education each month— served with two courses, wine, and dessert.

Strangers can be less open-minded. Some are patently rude: threatened by her spirit of experimentation. Boyfriends can often be impatient, scornful, embarrassed. Turned off by the whole "acting-out trip" as one put it, just before he walked away for good. If they can't handle it, good riddance!

By now, Stephanie's skin is crawling with revulsion. She has the feeling her story idea is nothing but self-indulgent tripe. *How will I ever learn to write something authentic and mean- ingful?* she wails silently.

She has the same inflamed feeling about her novel manuscript. She flinches every time she looks at it. She can feel her face flushing as if an audience is standing behind her; reading over her shoulder and laughing at her penny dreadful style.

She closes the file and sits with an absent stare. Her screen saver starts up and dances a techno light show across the screen. Stephanie wants to give up and go home. She wants to schlep back into the land of mediocrity: a land where nothing challenges her sense of identity the way writing does.

She thinks about the dirty laundry piling up and the pot-bound houseplants that need her attention. The checks she should be writing for almost-overdue bills. Right now, even paying bills seems like a pursuit more friendly than try- ing to be a writer. At least signing checks gets her somewhere on her scale of accomplishment. At least paying bills is con- structive and normal.

The man at the chessboard table is turning to a new page in his legal pad. Stephanie hears a crackle of paper, and looks up just in time to witness the fluid execution; the single, economical movement; the utter intensity of purpose. His pen hits the new page before the paper even has time to settle against the pad. Mr. Smith is on a roll.

Impulsively, Stephanie gets up and crosses the room. She pulls out the chair on the opposite side of the chessboard table and sits down. The seat is wicker and the chair back is erect; so erect she cannot sit comfortably. She leans forward against the table, puts her chin in one hand, and waits.

Mr. Smith continues to write. It's as if he is alone in the universe. Stephanie peers at the legal pad—burning with a desire to read the upside-down words. She's busy trying to decipher his handwriting when he raises his eyes.

"Yes?"

Mr. Smith's about thirty years old. His carrot-colored, silken hair is clipped close to his head. His eyes are blue. His lashes are so pale and golden they are only visible when he's looking down at his work. His skin is slightly red. It sports the remnants of a youth dominated by abundant freckles.

The mouth is suggestive. The lips are not full; and yet, something about the carnal shape of these thin lips suggests a closet hedonist. Now that he is looking at her, Stephanie feels her stomach flutter with excitement.

"Is this your name?" she asks, pointing to the coffee mug near his elbow.

"A smith is one who forges," he says. "I use words."

"Oh, I get it! Wordsmith."

He shrugs. "Perhaps."

Stephanie recognizes the rebuff, but she doesn't want to let go. "What's your name, then, if it's not Smith?"

"Is it any of your business?" His blue eyes test her.

"My name is Stephanie Handel," she offers hopefully.

"Good for you."

"You're trying to get rid of me," she accuses playfully.

"That *is* the plan." His pen taps the table as he looks

beyond her through the window. "You're impeding my work."

"I know." Stephanie is blushing but she doesn't want to leave yet. "I need your help."

"I don't have any help to give," he says, with a flick of the pen. "Don't even ask."

Stephanie's stunned, embarrassed, and mortified. She falls silent and watches as he goes back to his writing pad. But she knows in her bones this man has something to give her. She wants to slink under a rock and hide from the shame of his rejection but, at the same time, she can't tear herself away. She has to find a way to unlock the secret of Mr. Smith.

After a blank interlude she has an idea. She goes back to her work place to get her laptop and then returns to set it up on his table. She has to push a stack of used legal pads out of the way to make room for it. He ignores her and continues to write. Stephanie makes two more trips. She fetches her mug, her satchel, her notebook, and her cassette player; conveying them all to her new position at the chessboard table.

She's in.

Now that she's ensconced at his table, Stephanie feels self-conscious but elated. She knows Bridget is busy stealing curious glances and it makes her proud of her self-assertion. Stephanie has a hunch she has a long haul ahead of her, but she's high on the drug that this is something she needs to do.

Her new companion continues to write while emanating his inimitable body language: *Go away, world.*

Before asking for help again, Stephanie decides to try to win his trust. She opens the computer file for her novel and begins to fuss with it; hoping that her steady presence and the common goal of writing will eventually forge a bond between them. She ponders Mr. Smith's use of the word "forge" and promises herself she will use the word as a trigger for her next writing practice.

Right now, she's too unsettled to do anything but pretend to edit her manuscript. It's a passage she has edited repeatedly in the recent past. To move beyond this section involves the need to write fresh prose, but she's terrified she has nowhere to go with it.

She pecks at the keys. Refers at length to her thesaurus looking for precisely the right word for each alteration. It's depressing work. She almost loses her nerve and gives up the ground she has won by moving to the chessboard table. She's tempted to skulk away from this cold war, admit defeat, and go home.

After about thirty minutes, her writing partner comes to the end of his legal pad and has to start afresh on a brand new pad. He does this as if he's merely turning another page. Stephanie is suddenly aware that the pile of legals at the edge of the table is made up mostly of used pads. She studies their edges: realizes there are only two "virgins" left in the pile. The other six or seven have the buckled appearance of used paper.

"Is this a manuscript?" she ventures, gesturing at the stack of legals.

"Mm," he says, without looking up from the sentence he is writing.

Stephanie wonders then if her method of working on a computer using idea templates is too prudish. Here is someone who creates an entire manuscript by hand, on paper, and goes through legal pads as if planetary repercussions don't exist. Her smug belief in being "environmentally responsible" by using a laptop and Zip disks evaporates into a philosophic void. She thinks instead how his process is more organic than hers. Primal and free instead of uptight and technical.

As she glares at his manuscript pile and churns over these thoughts, she catches sight of the corner of an envelope protruding from the stack. Her next action goes against all of her mother's scrupulous training in manners and respect for the privacy of others—but she is consumed by a compulsive need to know. She pulls the envelope out and looks avidly at both addresses.

The return address is printed on an ivory label in gold lettering. The label reads "Stampfel Publishing House" and it gives a New York City street address. The delivery address is handwritten with a flourish to a post office box in Valdez; a tiny village about twenty minutes from town. Stephanie feels a bolt of recognition when she sees the name of the recipient: Dempsey Hewlett.

Dempsey Hewlett: up and coming young sci-fi genius. Two best-sellers under his belt; retail activity off the charts; rave reviews from every nook and cranny in creation.

As the thrill sinks in, she muses on his two smash hits. She'd read the first one last Christmas: *Babel Walk at Dawn*. It was so good, she promised herself she would buy the sequel the moment it hit the bookstores in Taos. She's already seen the reviews for *A Moment Bright and Hard*, so she knows the critics are raving that Mr. Hewlett has "outdone himself" with his second book. She has it on special order at Moby Dickens.

Her feeling of needing something from him increases. She watches him openly as he writes. Sensing her stare, his hand stops moving. He looks up at her and the brittle, cynical smile on his lips makes her heart lurch with fear. But he says nothing. Simply shakes his head and goes back to his work. Stephanie is relieved: He's letting her stay.

* * *

The following Friday, Stephanie shows up at Ranchos Coffee Co. a few minutes after opening time. It's almost 7:45 a.m. and the regulars are milling sociably before the workday gets going: tapping coffee from the air pots; greeting friends; waiting for an egg croissant or a breakfast burrito or a cream cheese bagel to go.

Dempsey's already enthroned. . . . He has possession of the chessboard table and looks as if he hasn't moved since the previous Friday. Deep into the act of creation, he notices nothing about the social scene around him. The radio is playing brisk, boppy Top 40 tunes from the stereo system on the shelf above his head—but even this doesn't seem to penetrate Dempsey's private bubble.

Stephanie feels conspicuous, but she forces herself to go ahead with her plan. She walks up boldly to his table, sets down her satchel, and then hoists her laptop into position in the table space he isn't using. Today his stack of pads rests on a chair he has pulled up beside him, so she has plenty of room to spread out.

Dempsey looks up briefly, sighs in mock exasperation, and goes straight back to his work. But even his irritation at her presence seems distant and absorbed—as though his level of concentration, so arcane and incorruptible, means that her puny existence barely registers in his cortex . . . let alone the deeper regions of his brain.

There is no sane reason for Stephanie to believe she can establish a rapport with this man. But her Sagittarian lust for risk-taking is in rocket propulsion mode: all set to jettison boosters and eject the payload into the Great Unknown. She can't bear to slow down now.

She knows Annalise would say, "What's really at work here, darlink, is your Sagittarian foolhardiness and stubborn pride." But Stephanie purposely has not unveiled the concept of Dempsey to Annalise. The last thing she wants to hear right now is sensible advice from a non-writer—best friend or not.

Stephanie gets out her writing practice notebook and places it on the closed lid of the laptop. After ordering a latté, she returns to the chessboard table and begins to write. She is using the word "forge" as a springboard into free association. She writes one page and then opens her laptop and boots into Windows. She wants to "blaze a trail" today. Clicking on her manuscript file, she scrolls to the paragraph she left hanging in Chapter Seven.

This morning Stephanie's determined to be pro-active

just like Dempsey. She sets herself a respectable goal—three pages—and begins to produce unpremeditated prose.

On one level, her plan is working well. She is creating new sentences and moving the story forward. But on another, less measurable level, Stephanie's going crazy. Hyper-aware of Dempsey sitting across the table, her curiosity about his work is eating a hole in her vital energy.

Finally, she pushes the computer to one side and folds her arms in front of her. She waits for Dempsey to interpret the signal and bestow his attention upon her.

Dempsey keeps her waiting for ten minutes. When he does look up, he's scowling.

"You have the concentration span of an infant."

"Can I read your manuscript?" she blurts, before he can break eye contact and re-engage with his legal pad.

Dempsey stares at her. It's as though Stephanie has asked him to remove his clothing and do the Highland fling. She squirms under his gaze. He is silent for so long, she can only take it as a "no." He fingers the handle of his coffee mug and roasts her slowly with his eyes. It's sheer torture, but she holds the stare. She is not willing to let him intimidate her.

"OK, if not, will you read mine?" she asks, with a dry mouth.

To her amazement, he holds out one hand. Stephanie dives into her satchel and retrieves the printout of her novel: chapters one to six. He takes it from her and tosses it onto the stack of legal pads on the chair next to his thigh.

"I need help," she says. She can feel herself gabbling but this looks like her one big chance. "I have terrible writer's block and my self-critic is so savage, I can barely work. I see you writing thousands of words every hour and I wonder how you got to be so free. Have you always been like this? Did you go to workshops or do a course in college? Do you enjoy writing? I feel as if I hate it, but it's in my blood. I usually feel so bad when I write, I just want to run away."

"Maybe you should," Dempsey responds languidly.

While she talks, his eyes wander the room . . . as if her words mean no more to him than a fly buzzing in his ear.

"Do you mean I should give up writing?" Stephanie asks, in awe and trepidation.

"I'm not your guru," he says, with some disgust.

He picks up his pen and goes back to his writing. After a moment, he appears to remember something relevant.

"You've got your own compass," he tells her, without looking up. "If you don't know how to use it then too bad."

"A compass?" Stephanie urges. "What do you mean—a compass?"

But Dempsey refuses to answer. His head is down and he's already working at his usual steady pace. Stephanie gives up and goes back to her manuscript. She is feeling confused, grumpy, and cheated of a secret worth having.

She meets her goal of three pages by eleven a.m. She stops to have a turkey sandwich with sun-dried tomato pesto on fresh panini bread. The turkey is succulent and the pesto is rich and decadent. The corn chips that come with her lunch are the cheesy kind; the kind she hates. Dempsey watches her furtively to see if she'll eat them. When she doesn't, he starts to munch. He polishes off her chips—along with the orange segment and the dill pickle.

"You're wasting the best parts," Dempsey mumbles, with his mouth full.

"Writing kills my appetite," she says miserably, pushing her plate away.

Stephanie is on the verge of tears. She doesn't want to break down in front of Dempsey, but her heart is strangled as if she's in mourning for someone dear. The three pages she completed before lunch ache in her chest. More sludge—deep, fetid, sodden sludge. Stephanie watches Dempsey work for a few more moments and then packs up her satchel and leaves without a goodbye. Dempsey doesn't even glance up.

* * *

Stephanie's Saturdays are devoted to running errands and doing household chores. In an attempt to blot out her failure from the previous day, she buries herself in the minutiae of maintaining her lifestyle. Desperately, she hits the town with Annalise on Saturday night—in search of a few more of those elusive hours of forgetfulness.

Together, they discover that the social scene in Taos has struck a lukewarm patch. The interesting people are all busy doing something else. They try Eske's Brew Pub; they try L.B.'s; they try the cocktail bar in Doc Martin's restaurant at the Taos Inn. They even try the lounge at the Holiday Inn but with no luck. By 9 p.m. the night has completely fizzled. They decide to go home and play the new poker game Annalise has just been taught.

Stephanie acts depressed the whole evening. Annalise purposely doesn't ask her why. There are certain times when Annalise just wants to veg out and "let things slide." She holds a responsible position in loans at the south branch of People's Bank and, by the end of the week, she feels drained. In such a ratty mood herself, Annalise definitely doesn't want to listen to Stephanie dredge up her stupid writer's angst again. She just wants to drink a beer and indulge in some juicy Taoseño gossip. Anything to cheer up and forget her working blues.

Recognizing the "just don't go there" mood, Stephanie doesn't try to unburden herself to Annalise. They keep communications strictly at surface level; ending the evening early with a shot of Kahlua sipped slowly in a weary silence.

Traditionally, Stephanie spends Sunday with her family. After a day of hiking or yard work, they wind up the weekend with a late-afternoon barbecue on her parents' patio in Arroyo Seco. The intimate mood of family togetherness swells in harmony with the vastness of blue skies and rolling mesa.

Stephanie loves her mother and father, and she's also close to her Aunt Wendy who lives next door to them in Seco. Wendy has a new husband by the name of Arnold and, so far, so good, he fits right in. Dale and Jackie—Wendy's children by her first marriage and Stephanie's favorite cousins—often join them on the patio with their respective spouses, children, babies, and dogs.

Dale is a popular journalist with *The Taos News*. Dale and Stephanie love to talk shop—although they have radically different takes on writing.

Jackie is a silversmith. She designs and makes jewelry which she sells both locally and nationally. Her work is widely sought after and respected; her name synonymous with good taste and Southwestern chic.

One lazy Sunday afternoon, Stephanie had attempted to explain her writer's block to these dear friends. She could tell as she talked she was missing the mark. Being artisans who make a living from their craft, Dale and Jackie are accustomed to commercialism and productivity under pressure.

Dale tried the hardest to comprehend. In an effort to help his favorite cousin, he made hard-hitting suggestions on how to "break through."

"Keep hacking at it until you have some copy, Steph," he urged. "Then cultivate the pearl within the dross."

Jackie responded with a vague smile and sympathetic noises. She clearly did not understand Stephanie's feelings on this. Stephanie kicked herself mentally and vowed, in future, to leave relatives out of her private torment.

This particular Sunday she's feeling like a hermit. She cannot picture doing folksy things with the family today. She would have to don a social veneer and fake a positive attitude. Either that, or let it all hang out and risk probing family questions about her "deplorable frame of mind."

Stephanie knows, from experience, it is impossible to conceal anything of significance from her mother and father.

Aunt Wendy also has a good radar for emotional submarines. Social veneer is not going to cut it with this family.

She feels too delicate to field probing questions and too depressed to deal with kids and babies and dogs. Even the Enchanted Circle drive through Angel Fire her father wants to do today no longer sounds inviting. Stephanie gets out of bed for five minutes to phone her mother and plead a migraine. Then she sleeps until noon and wakes up entrenched in self-loathing.

With an empty Sunday afternoon stretching ahead of her, Stephanie feels guilty about her writing. She knows she should be using this uncommitted block of time to make progress with her novel, but she's too numb to be creative. Dimly, she realizes she's having an identity crisis or maybe a nervous breakdown.

Am I a writer? I don't know. Do I want to continue trying to be a writer? I don't know. Maybe not.

She washes her hair with a new herbal shampoo, has a B.L.T. with cilantro for brunch, then drifts through a magazine article from *Condé Nast Traveler*.

Essaouira, the jewel of Morocco, looks like a place of wholesome integrity. Humble men in burnooses make their simple living selling seafood and spices in the marketplace. Stephanie admires the vivid photography. She can't help but notice that the engraved Moroccan teapots hung from hooks in the quaint little antique shop emanate more character and functionality than her own abysmal life does.

Still feeling drugged from too much sleep, Stephanie flips through endless photo albums; passively reliving twenty-eight years of her life. But today her most treasured memories seem tarnished and seedy. The course she's taken in life and the decisions she's made seem hollow, self-serving, and crass.

She needs something less inward and more physical to kill the time, so she experiments with her new Basia Gold electric hair removal system. The slender, pink, femininelyshaped device looks benign, but its 24-karat gold-plated disks whir with sinister precision—pulling her ankle, shin, knee and thigh hair out by the roots. The operation feels like a multitude of tiny bee stings. Grimacing, Stephanie barbers one section at a time with resentful determination.

By the time she's done with her hair removal project, the afternoon has progressed to the verge of dusk. Although the sunset is shaping up to be a stunner, Stephanie lowers the Venetian blinds. Her legs are peppered with a mass of angry, red pores. Her skin feels violated. When she checks her legs in the full-length mirror, she feels ugly and cheap.

There's nowhere left to turn. She has run out of aimless, solitary ways to fill her time. She wanders into the living room to browse through her bookshelf.

Despite her voracious love of reading, today she has no desire to begin a new novel. She has no desire, either, to read more of the luminous *How to Think Like Leonardo da Vinci: Seven Steps to Genius Every Day* by Michael J. Gelb— the young, handsome, successful, integrated-looking expert on accelerated learning and leadership development.

Reading books will only remind her that she's a failed author. Leonardo da Vinci reminds her that she's only a moth while he is the flame of brilliance. She flutters to oblivion on a Sunday at dusk while Leonardo radiates on the page with his clever inventions, his prodigious designs, his artistic masterpieces, and his finely tuned sense of the infinite. Even the tale of his legendary stupendous dinner party debacle makes her feel like a pathetic slug stuck fast in its own slime.

She goes to bed early and lies awake for what feels to Stephanie like two-thirds of the night.

* * *

Stephanie's appointment book is full. She drags herself out of bed on Monday morning and into her tailored business suit.

Most of her consultant calls this week are routine follow-ups with satisfied clients. Her clients don't seem to notice her low energy. She smiles by rote and neglects her usual peppy public relations lingo, but her clients enjoy her presence and her "expertise" without picking up on the clues.

This week, Stephanie lets good networking leads go cold. And when she calls on two prospective clients, she blows her lines and forgets to leave her business card. Somehow, though, everyone is still happy by Thursday evening—the end of her formal working week.

She forces herself to do her usual Thursday wind-up: calling every client in her card file in preparation for another week of doing business. In the process, she picks up a new lead fed to her by Georgio; her inside contact at the Chamber of Commerce.

To her surprise, both the prospective clients from her sloppy footwork sign up for a full consultant's package. She's clearly reaping the power of the testimonials in her brochure. It's a small town and word of mouth is paramount. The word around town about Stephanie Handel is: "She gets results."

This week, the popularity she enjoys and the respect she inspires among the local business owners makes her feel like a phony. If they saw me drowning in my own puddle of drama they wouldn't be quite so impressed, she thinks, when her work of strategic phone calls is over for another week.

Out of habit, she has finalized her working week a day early to leave herself that one precious day in which to write. Friday, her day of creative risk and true aspiration. . . .

Maybe I won't use my Friday for writing this week, she muses sluggishly. Maybe I'll cruise down to Ojo Caliente and soak my ulcerated ego in the hot springs. Mummify myself in a head-to-toe mud-pack. Escape into a full-body massage with warm towels, essential oils, and ambient music.

She decides to sleep on it.

In the morning, Stephanie wakes at 10 a.m., looks at

the clock, and decides she has already blown her day. She languishes in bed for another hour and then stands brooding in a hot shower for twenty-five minutes. She puts on her oldest, shabbiest jeans and the black L.A. logo T-shirt she has always hated—the same one Annalise thinks is "swank." She doesn't care what she looks like today.

With no forethought, and feeling chronically disconnected from herself, Stephanie checks her satchel, slips her *Rhythms of the Chakras* tape into a side pocket, picks up her laptop, puts it down again, and then goes to the car without it. She knows she's on her way to Ranchos Coffee Co. but feels as if she doesn't much care. The laptop is too heavy today and she doesn't want to lug it. Even the satchel seems pretentious in her nihilistic, self-destructive mood.

What I need is some tranquilizers or some cheap, rotgut booze, she thinks—not a prissy satchel full of my deep and meaningful B.S.

Dempsey is seated at the chessboard table writing like a champ. Stephanie trudges to his table, fumbles a chair into position and sits down. She doesn't even want latté today. She sits like a person suffering from shock: staring ahead but not seeing what's in front of her. Dempsey glances at her but says nothing. His writing pace falters imperceptibly.

After ten or fifteen minutes of this amorphous, groggy atmosphere, Dempsey gets up and pulls her some Columbian Roast from the air pot. She drinks robotically from the paper cup—not tasting the acid of black coffee; not registering that Dempsey has made a friendly overture for once.

An hour goes by, and Stephanie can feel herself begin to thaw out from her personal Ice Age. She listens to the *Dead Can Dance* CD playing on the stereo and feels her blood take on the haunting urgency of the songs. She orders a latté and starts to think about her writing practice notebook.

Now and then, Dempsey throws her a curious look between his marathon engagements with the page. Stephanie zeroes in on the undercurrent. . . . Dempsey's actually waiting in suspense to see what she will do next. She opens her notebook and writes the first thing which comes to mind.

> *If I could work the way Dempsey works, I know my life would sparkle instead of wallowing in despair. He's a mystic; a swallower of stationery; a Rasputin of the page.*
>
> *Carrying a flaming torch, he wades unfrightened into the sewers of his writing— kicking aside the sewer rats and flicking off the cockroaches as he goes.*
>
> *Nothing stops him. There is no sludge thick enough to slow him down; no foulness in the sewers overwhelming enough to discourage him from his path. He chooses to be in the sewers: Embracing the journey, he feasts on the gassy by-products and inhales the malodorous biosphere with relish.*
>
> *Dempsey has a writer's compass and he knows how to use it. He may stray down side alleys or fall down unlit shafts, but he always knows how to find the manhole and break through into daylight. His discipline is the discipline of a wild thing.*
>
> *With his ferocious growl and hackles on end, monsters of the sewer blunder aside to let him pass. He is so intent on his prey, he doesn't notice the raw stamina he exerts. It is his natural state of being.*
>
> *Dempsey has the survival skills to be a writer. If a sewer rat bit off his right hand he would simply go on writing with his left.*

Stephanie marvels at her creation. Proofreading the passage, she likes what she's written. Miraculously, writing about the sludge has siphoned it from her mood: She feels her strength returning. Dempsey notices her revival.

"Burn rubber, Stephanie," he says, dryly amused.

Stephanie pretends not to hear him. For once, *she* is the writer on fire—the one hitting light speed in her own private time capsule while deaf to conversation and blind to her environment. She applies herself to the paper again to write another page. This time she puts herself in the sewer to see how she will cope.

By the end of that second page, Stephanie knows she has made a mistake. She is lost in the sewer with no torch and no compass. Somehow, in the darkness and the stench, she knows the next available manhole is at least a hundred miles away. The rush of bliss and power she'd felt on the first page is gone.

She has finally written something she really likes. But, the "acceptable" passage—the one about Dempsey the Fearless—amounts to only a page. A mere page: two hundred and seventeen words. A fraction of a mile along the perpetual trek into crude wilderness on the way to becoming a "real" writer.

Still hanging on by a fingernail, Stephanie attempts to list her own set of survival skills.

> *A love of words, of reading, of invented characters and a good story line. An imagination that gives me no rest. A flexible lifestyle with time to write. A laptop I know how to use. Parents who want to see me live my dream. A pristine mountain setting to inspire me.*

It's all too pitiful. Stephanie is acutely aware that these are not "skills" she's listing. These are assets, bonuses, perks of the job. Cushy benefits in a harsh world; like a spoiled rich girl pretending to rough it in a satin tent.

> *What would I do if a sewer rat bit off my writing hand? Contract septicemia from the gutter germs? Scream wordlessly for help that never comes? Die of exposure and loss of blood? (Ah, the perfect excuse not to write!)*
> *Meanwhile, Dempsey sloshes past me in the tunnel. He puts down another 2,000 words of award-winning prose before my body's fully cold.*

It's getting close to 4 p.m.—the afternoon rush is on. Bridget and her assistant, Larry, choreograph their movements at the espresso machine; each attempting to serve multiple customers. The cash drawer is replete. Larry's somewhat slower than Bridget and he slops cappuccino foam, but business is booming. People are spending their money and kicking back in the conversation corner with their caffeine. Behaving as though time is not a luxury. Projecting an image that life was *not* designed for pitting oneself against failure on an hourly basis.

Stephanie has reached saturation point with her own narcissism. Negative narcissism, certainly—not vanity or self-love—but just as cloying and tedious. . . . In fact, more so, she tells herself. At least true narcissism is about *desire*.

Dempsey can tell by her restlessness that she's about to abandon her writing and go home. He puts his palms together under his chin in prayerful repose; bowing his head in Zen-like respect for the elemental polarities of flow.

"Congratulations," he says. "You did it."

Stephanie laughs without mirth.

"Yep. I made it out of bed this morning. Whoopee."

Shutting her notebook, she returns her dirty latté mug

to the counter. Bridget and Larry salute her from the trenches as they stand knee-deep in a wave of consumerism. When she returns to the table for her satchel and keys, Stephanie is surprised to find Dempsey waiting for her—consciously divorced from his work and fully present in the land of the living.

He is holding a creased half-sheet of paper with pencil markings on one side. He looks like a public speaker waiting to give an important speech: marshalling quotes and rehearsing punch lines in his head.

"It's Kachina Road," he says, handing her the paper. "If you get lost, call me from the pay phone at the tavern. But don't talk to the locals. The locals in Valdez are territorial to the point of litigation."

She squints at the pencil markings until she finally gets it. He is talking about an invitation to the inner sanctum! She is looking at a map to his house. His telephone number is written in pen beneath a rudimentary sketch of the village.

"I see you wondering: Is this a dinner invitation? *No*," Dempsey informs her sternly. "Don't expect to be fed. I won't be home from work until six-thirty so don't bother to show up before seven. I always take a shower after work."

Stephanie is embarrassed at this personal revelation. The pedestal which Dempsey occupies has no bathroom sink, no shower, no toilet, and no bed. She can visualize him in a sewer but not with bodily functions of his own.

"OK," she says, wishing to heck her voice didn't sound so froggy and unsure. "Sevenish. See you then."

Dempsey tips his chair and looks mischievous.

"*And* . . . I wouldn't mess with Mrs. Magillacuddy if I were you," he adds.

"Who's Mrs. Magillacuddy?"

"She's the unofficial soup kitchen of Taos and brave surrogate mother to psychotic orphans such as myself."

Stephanie waits for more information. Dempsey only smiles enigmatically. He waves a dismissal with his left hand while returning to his sentence structure with the right. It's as if she went "poof" and disappeared. Stephanie is befuddled to be left standing like a ghost. She turns on her heel and leaves.

Even alone at home, this strange turn of events still has her off balance. Stephanie looks in the mirror to assess her appearance. In her thrift store jeans, unkempt ponytail, and crumpled T-shirt, she looks like a woman who doesn't give a damn. She toys with possible wardrobe upgrades for a while—until she realizes that any improvement whatsoever will signal "date."

Am I attracted to Dempsey?

She asks this of herself while gazing in the mirror.

Am I hoping for romance?

Stephanie doesn't know how to sort the man/woman sexual vibes from the writer/ego issues. Sitting at Dempsey's exclusive table definitely comes loaded with its own electric nuances. . . . But how much of it is purely the lust of reflected glory from Dempsey's fame and success?

She checks off points in her mind:

Dempsey dresses with absent-minded inattention to color, style, and trend. He drives a dusty Oldsmobile with expired tags and still prefers to write everything by hand. Instead of parading his books on the talk-show circuit, he writes alone, day by day, in an obscure coffeehouse in northern New Mexico.

For Stephanie, the glory of basking in his fame has nothing to do with the trappings of success. For her, it's about the affirmation of talent: the public sanctioning of his books; the green light on his creativity. Things she wants for herself. Dempsey has a vast, admiring audience. . . . Surely, this is the most fundamental reason to soldier on through the sewers; cockroaches or not.

Stephanie rakes the elastic band from her ponytail and fluffs out her hair.

"Do I want Dempsey to want me?" she ponders out

loud to her reflection.

Her feelings are muddled and no clear answer comes. She *does* know she wants Dempsey to read her manuscript. To caress her with his approval. To supply her with her own fundamental reason to soldier on.

Dempsey's approval would be the ultimate coition for her right now. The uplift of orgasm without the sex. An explosion of life force enough to resuscitate her paralytic heart and propel her into the realms of Tantric writing.

Her clothes are sweaty and she decides to change as a matter of comfort. She chooses a low-key outfit and applies the safest shade of pink lipstick she can find. She aims to look professional but unassuming.

Sex and writing: units in a metaphysical nucleus—a continuum—not something she can isolate, control or predict. She can, however, elect to show up at Dempsey's house looking well-groomed and alive to her own destiny.

At 6:45, she sets out for Valdez. The view across the mesa is infused with magenta light. The sunflowers massed along Blueberry Hill Road catch at her senses. Taos Mountain is there, brooding beyond the traffic lights on Highway 522, offering self-realization and transcendence. As she drives the section of NM-150 near the base of the peak, Stephanie tries not to be overpowered by the mountain's cosmic rootedness and the message of simplicity flowing from it.

If only she could embrace these qualities herself, then the mountain wouldn't daunt her. Locals are supposed to be blasé about the mountain. Only newbies and tourists wax religious about its mythic potency.

The road to Dempsey's house turns out to be more of a challenge than she feels up to. There are no street signs in the tiny village of Valdez, and Dempsey's pencil has smudged at a crucial point on the map. The tavern pumps music as the scruffy clientele wander the parking lot or talk to their drunk friends sitting in battered pickups.

As she crawls past looking for Kachina Road, groups of men nursing cans of Budweiser and hand-rolled cigarettes leer at her. When she has to pass them three times due to wrong turns, the men snigger and call out saucy propositions. Stephanie does *not* want to stop and use the pay phone.

On her fourth turn, she happens up the correct side road and locates the first landmark mentioned on the map. She uses her odometer to track the 3.7 miles the map tells her she must go from there. The dirt road is a nightmare of deep potholes, loose gravel, churned-up mud, and eroding banks. She's climbing almost a thousand feet above Taos: leaving behind the Valdez Valley for the foothills of the Sangre de Cristo Mountains.

By the time she pulls down the long driveway with the wooden sign marked Casa del Sol, her legs are trembling from the stressful drive.

"This is just so *Taos*," Annalise would have smirked, had she accompanied Stephanie on this interesting journey.

The property Dempsey lives on is dense with juniper and piñon and a smattering of cedar. The air is fragrant with the scent of evergreen at high altitude. A large, jolly woman in a print dress and sandals watches her get out of the car.

The woman had not been out on the front stoop when Stephanie first drove up. It seems she timed her emergence to look coincidental. It strikes Stephanie as creepy and bizarre— as if this woman has been waiting at a peephole for the arrival of The Visitor.

Two large dogs loll at her feet and thump their bushy tails in the dust around the ornamental cactus bed. A gray cat poised on the latilla fence eyes Stephanie balefully. She can't quite determine whether this is a welcoming committee or a platoon of Dempsey's private guards. The woman does look friendly . . . but bossy and ready to interfere. Stephanie has no way to avoid an interaction.

"You must be Steph," the woman asserts comfortably,

as in "a fact is a fact is a fact." The abbreviation of her name strikes Stephanie as off-kilter. Dempsey has never once called her Steph.

"Me, I'm Karen McGindle," she goes on. "Dempsey's landlord. He don't get visitors. Gets alota checks in the mail but no visitors. For all his filthy moolah, that boy lives like a sainted monk. Them checks never even make it to the bank—unless I do the deposits m'self."

Stephanie steps forward; lets Mrs. McGindle take her hand. The handshake is sloppy and lasts much too long for Stephanie's peace of mind. She feels as if she's smothering in Karen McGindle's pushy aura.

"That sweet thing," McGindle prattles. "He just don't care about the necessities of life. Never seen anything like it. Lucky he lives here with me or that boy'd starve to death with a pen in his hand. He'd live on Ritz crackers and coffee if I didn't cook him a square meal once a day. Even have to buy toilet paper for 'im." She shakes her head in disbelief at such willing austerity. "He lives for his writin'. Reminds me of that coke addict, James—my upstairs tenant before Demps. Only difference is: Demps snorts lines of words 'steada cocaine."

Stephanie feels awash in intimate details she's almost too afraid to absorb. She is even deeper in awe of Dempsey's dedication to his writerdom. She can't imagine going without toilet paper or regular meals just so she can write. In fact, in that moment, Stephanie cannot think of a single sacrifice she makes in order to create a bubble of her own to write in.

McGindle catches the bewildered look on her face.

"Didn't mean to alarm you, honey-bun," she corrects herself hastily. "Dempsey is a good boy. A real hard worker. And not the least bit uppity about his success. Those ol' interviewers from the city—they call him up all the time hoping for quotes. But, he uses that dreadful language of his to get rid of 'em. Calls 'em 'parasites making a livin' off the real McCoys.' He says a real writer is up in the garret workin'—not feastin' on the spoils of capitalism."

What little courage Stephanie arrived with shrivels to a curd of inadequacy. If she could fade off into the trees and escape, she would. She knows Annalise would be laughing her head off if she could be here to see Stephanie in another self-induced pickle.

"Where is all your famous Sagittarian charisma now, girlfriend?" Annalise would gloat. "Where's that golden P.R. tongue of yours when you need it?"

Karen McGindle draws breath for her next verbal on-slaught at the same instant Dempsey appears at the rail of his second-story front porch.

"Aw, have a heart, Mrs. M," he scolds affectionately. "Don't talk her into the grave on her first visit."

Stephanie is flustered by this hint that she might become a regular visitor. She covers her embarrassment with a gummy smile and a falsetto hello to Dempsey. She is relieved and grateful when he waves her impatiently up the stairs and then herds her through the door like a small child.

"Do you need a glass of water after your ordeal, dear?" he says acidly, taking in Stephanie's white face. "You look as if Mrs. Magillacuddy put a hex on you. She's really a harmless old mother hen, you know. A monumental busy-body—true—but a sweetie nevertheless. She's the one who makes sure I get some nutrition in my diet."

Stephanie gapes around and is bombarded firsthand by the reality of Dempsey's lifestyle. His apartment goes beyond "minimalist" into wanton deprivation. The living room has only a chain store do-it-yourself table and a desk chair on roller wheels with one plastic armrest missing. The table is messy with legal pads, reference books, Manila folders, and other writing tools. The carpet under the window is thick with dead flies and the overhead light bulb is naked.

Compulsively, Stephanie is drawn from room to room in housekeeping horror and fascinated pity. The kitchen nook is scantily equipped: odds and ends from a set of blue plastic picnic ware; an electric coffee percolator; a bag of gingersnap cookies; a collection of coffee-stained porcelain mugs.

The bedroom comes complete with a futon mattress thrown on the floor and a cardboard box of jumbled clothing. The bathroom has one threadbare towel, a can of lime shaving foam, a toothbrush, and a stash of unwashed coffee mugs.

Dempsey's back balcony—with its panoramic view of mesa, mountains, and the distant, snaking yawn of the Rio Grande gorge—is the only over-furnished space in the entire apartment. The 6' x 3' area is jammed with two mildewed lawn chairs and a dead houseplant in a clay pot. Stephanie is not surprised to find a huddle of abandoned coffee cups lurking underneath the lawn chairs and behind the clay pot.

The view at this time of the day is tender and ethereal. Pulling herself away with an effort, she turns to see Dempsey foraging through the litter of writing material on his table; ostensibly looking for something specific. But he is easily sidetracked from his task and lingers at length over one distraction after another. Stephanie takes one more ravenous look at the magnificent sunset before returning to the living room.

There is no sofa, and Dempsey is sitting on the only chair available inside the apartment. So Stephanie sits on the floor with her back against the wall and waits for the motive behind his invitation to be revealed.

After the boredom of studying Dempsey's dead flies and grimy, smeared windows has stolen the final ounce of energy from her limbs, Dempsey makes a sharp movement and throws something on the floor at her feet.

It's her manuscript.

Stephanie cringes and waits for the fatal thrust of his critique. All hope of a literary orgasm drains from her soul as she watches him swivel ninety degrees in his Wal-Mart office chair to confront her.

"Don't worry," he says, graciously divining her sense

of dread. "I didn't read your thing. I only took it so you'd clam up and let me get back to what I was doing."

Stephanie blushes and ducks her head low. Dempsey slaps his leg hard as if that's what it takes to get her to listen. His voice becomes loud and belligerent.

"I *know* what you want." His index finger lunges in accusation. "You want me to christen you. You want Dempsey to knight you with that magic wand that says 'Stephanie's a writer.' D'you really think I know what I'm doing just because I have something in print? You think I don't have self-doubt the way you do? No. . . . The only thing I really 'know' in life is that a writer is someone who does it. Someone who wakes up and puts words on the page every day."

"But you're a *good* writer," she argues in a tiny voice, struggling hard to hold onto her composure. "You have a true vocation for it. Your stories are riveting. Your reviews are sublime. You even make money at it!"

"Y'know something, angel?" Dempsey says harshly. "I'm a writer because I don't have any impressive skills to put on a résumé. I haven't got what it takes to be a doctor or an attorney or a computer programmer. I am a high school drop out and a barbarian. My social skills suck. I hate women and I hate most men. You could've figured *that* one out for yourself if you weren't so damn naive and gullible. Maybe you're too 'nice' to be a writer, Stephanie. Writers deal with the savage side of humanity—if you don't already know that. You have to get some blood on your hands. Some spit on your pen. Nice is not risky. Nice is not maddened with creator's disease. Nice is a big, fat, disgusting cop-out. Nice writers finish last."

Stephanie is devastated to the core. She can't stumble down Dempsey's shadowy staircase fast enough.

Moths swarm the patio floodlight. Karen McGindle is in a three hundred pound squat petting her dogs on the front stoop; almost completely blocking the path Stephanie must take to reach the car. Mrs. McGindle looks up expectantly, but

Stephanie blows past with tears flying from her cheeks and sobs choking her in a violent spasm of deathly heartbreak.

It does not matter that "Mrs. McGillacuddy" has witnessed her humiliation. Stephanie plans never to come within sight of Casa del Sol for the rest of her miserable life.

She drives recklessly on the treacherous road; nearly hitting an elk while coming around a sharp curve in the dusky piñon forest. Back on the pavement in the village of Valdez, the tears which blur her vision distort the drunken antics outside the tavern into a scene from a delusional dream.

The hurt is real and so painful she has no way to block it. The sounds coming from her nose and mouth horrify her with their primitiveness.

She is climbing out of the Valdez Valley. At the top of the cliff, she hangs a left onto the deserted Rim Road and heads for the Ski Valley—driving like a speed demon with no sensibility of danger. She is taking the hairpin curves way too fast; using the opposite lane to cut corners . . . inviting final deliverance from her betrayed and broken spirit.

When she reaches the Blissful Summit restaurant, she pulls off the road and finds a secluded place in the parking lot beneath a spreading tree. The restaurant is closed for the off-season and the building is dark.

Stephanie flips on the interior light and gropes for the box of travel tissues. It takes her several minutes to blow her nose and she uses up most of the box.

Slumped submissively after the wild aggression of her flight and still waiting for the wracking of her sobs to settle, she gradually tunes into the manuscript restrained in its rubber bands on the passenger seat beside her. Her first impulse is to toss it into the Rio Hondo flowing a few yards away.

She knows Dempsey did not read one word of it. Still, Stephanie feels as if she's been submitted to a verdict on the merits of her writing: A verdict she has no way to survive.

Apathy, grief, and hopelessness permeate the stale,

compartmentalized air. Stephanie rolls down her window and ponders the passage she had penned earlier that day about Dempsey's survival skills. Ponders Dempsey Hewlett's piercing blue eyes and his collection of dirty coffee cups. Ponders Mrs. McGindle keeping him alive with home-cooked meals so he can write like a deranged drug addict; royalty checks piling up unheeded on the doorstep.

As the images convulse in her mind and build to a crescendo, the hurt turns to a rush of fury. She scrabbles in the glove box for a pen. Her notebook is at home, still tucked inside her satchel, and she has no blank paper here in the car. Stephanie seizes her manuscript, whips it over, snaps off the rubber band, and begins to write on the back of the last page of chapter six.

> *Dempsey: A cruel, privileged condor perched on a dead branch surveying the world. He despises all that he sees and is rewarded for his hatred. Other creatures feed him but he gives no thanks. He pours his vitriol on their offerings; marinating the free meat in the astringent of his selfishness before tearing it apart with his immortalized beak.*
>
> *Dempsey's life on the savanna is devoid of beauty or grace. The condor is king of a solitaire domain. As long as he admits no other to his private world, his reign can never be challenged or usurped.*
>
> *The condor is a coward—even while he screeches in scorn at the cowardice of his victims. He flexes supple claws on the dead branch: convinced he reigns supreme.*
>
> *The condor feasts on the vulnerability of others . . . the rotting flesh of the weak who cannot prevail.*

It feels so good to ravage the page with her emotions.

With her manuscript tilted and wedged against the steering wheel, Stephanie finds the physical act of writing a challenge at first. But once she's warmed up, nothing matters except the act of expression. She uses a flashlight when it becomes too dark to see her words.

After the condor, she shifts gears and does a personal narrative based on Dempsey and her recent experiences reeling in his slipstream. The account is thick with her feelings: She takes it beyond any realm of objectivity into a slanderous wallow in the mud. His character is trampled and trashed—nothing Dempsey says or does is defensible in her eyes. She derives great pleasure from being as malicious as she can be. There is no pedestal in sight.

Her hand becomes cramped, but she doesn't want to omit anything. She describes the café where they write; the road to Dempsey's house; his landlord and her dogs; the barren apartment; DH's brilliant career; his scathing blue eyes.

Just before midnight, Stephanie quits writing to drive home beneath a New Mexican sky peppered with a sackful of stars. Despite her aroused mental state and chaotic emotions, she falls asleep easily and wakes refreshed at 7 a.m.

She gets out of bed with single-minded intent.

By 8 a.m., she's pulling up in front of Ranchos Coffee Co. with her laptop, her satchel, her music, and her ambition. Anger fuels her actions. She knows her smoldering desire to prove herself to Dempsey is childish and overblown, but she doesn't give a damn. She's self-righteous and imposing; energetic and controlled. Stephanie is tall and erect as she enters the room.

She is pleased and somewhat smug to find her favorite table next to the Moorish door unoccupied. She sees it as a little dab of kismet coming her way. Stephanie offloads her writing equipment and walks to the counter. She orders her latté and chooses a fresh biscotti—all while keeping her face averted from the sacred cow sitting at the chessboard table.

Dempsey is stationed at his "desk," rock solid as ever, working diligently. To look his way would be an admission of defeat; a sign of weakening; an appeal for attention and approval. From now on, Stephanie's determined to be ruthless.

With her beloved latté and her macadamia-studded vanilla biscotti, she makes herself at home at her table by the window and then leisurely reviews her outpourings from the night before. Instead of reviling what she has written, she is struck by the potential of the raw material laid out before her like a palette of unmixed paints. . . . Material enough for a novel about an introverted, acerbic writer. A novel with Taos Mountain as the backdrop and the wild sage of the mesa as the dominating aroma. A story of professional jealousy and betrayal set in her own backyard.

The main character—the arrogant but dysfunctional writer—will be modeled on Dempsey. She will let the intensity of her emotions give the story a chime of credibility. The explosive germ of Dempsey's prickly nature will be buried in an introverted fictional character she'll use her native wits and imagination to invent.

Is it healthy to let my obsession with Dempsey shape my work like this? she wonders, in a familiar wave of terror and ambiguity.

Stephanie reminds herself the *subject* is not the issue. As long as she is writing with passion, she's doing the writing she was born to do. She reminds herself that, once she's written the virus of Dempsey Hewlett out of her immune system, she can go ahead and write whatever comes next.

Her laptop has never had so much enthusiastic traffic on its keys. Writer's block and loss of self-worth for every sentence she puts down are nothing but dull memories from her safe and comfortable past.

She's on the cutting edge: writing from her gut; slicing her way through the sewers with a gleaming machete and a flaming Olympic torch. She passes Dempsey in a whoosh of Spartan athletics; leaving him paddling and doodling in her wake.

By now, it is almost 3 o'clock, and she's forgotten to stop for lunch. Inadvertently, Stephanie glances up from her work; her eyes are drawn to the chessboard table. Dempsey's hand moves across the page in fearsome virtue while a smile hovers on his lean, sensuous lips.

Almost like a telegraph which brings arresting news, Dempsey's smile instinctively gives her the score. . . .

Dempsey has done her a "favor" with his cruel words. He planned his strategy and then lured Stephanie to the most effective setting for her initiation. He applied shock therapy to a fellow writer to bring her to her feet.

Perhaps Dempsey has a writing guru who once helped him in the same way. Did Dempsey suffer degradation at the hands of his own personal literary idol?

Maybe someday she will ask him if her guru hunch is correct. Right now, Stephanie doesn't waste her time on gratitude. Her heart is not melting with appreciation for Dempsey the Good Samaritan. She is too busy concocting delicious scenarios to portray her character's cold and selfish nature, his unwholesome, monkish lifestyle, and his snide and sanctimonious tongue.

She decides to name her writer Linus Condor-Jones. She's tickled with the choice and delighted with herself. She visualizes Linus with a condor's head, scaring away his fans at a book signing event in New York City, and giggles. Dempsey looks her way and she holds up her mug in a toast to condors.

She has forgotten that today is Saturday: her day for groceries and domestic chores. Writing has become a rich and entertaining snow scene inside a private bubble. Turned upside down, the bubble becomes a thing of magic and desire; a static tableau bursting to life with the free-spirited snowflakes swirling up the fun.

Taos Mountain is not visible from the picture window of the coffeehouse. But in the dim reaches of her pure creative ego, Stephanie knows the sacred mountain is out there in the sunshine chuckling and enjoying the switcheroo.

FERTILE MATERIAL

DRUNK WITH POWER You are the all-powerful Roman god looking down from above. You know you can manipulate these pitiful creatures known as "human beings" like helpless pawns on a planet-size chessboard. You decide to teach one of these insufferable ninnies a lesson. How do you go about it? Will you make yourself known to your victim? What do the other gods think of your craftiness and razor-sharp wit?

DREAMS YOU NEVER DREAMED OF Cecile Wunjo is an intuitive tarot reader, astrologer, and numerology expert. Each morning, she competently recalls her dreams from the night before and records them in the special dream journal she's been keeping for years. You're an accountant and a light, dreamless sleeper—an insomniac who's never attained REM in your entire life. You're madly envious of Cecile and badly want to keep your own dream journal. . . . In fact, you want it so bad you're prepared to lie. Write three dreams to show off to Cecile. Use the fancy journal you found in a New Age store.

MUCHO MACHO & THE FLUFFY SLIPPER Rugged Bruce Ballioh is a man's man's man. Describe his vehicle, his hobbies, his toolshed, his profession. Then write about Didi Dearlove: the ultra-feminine gal in the pink convertible. How does Ms. Dearlove spend her time? What's her motto in life? And what happens when Didi and Bruce meet?

FERTILE MATERIAL UNLIMITED

MORE FERTILE MATERIAL

THE KISSING REFLEX You are in the third grade; your teacher's name is Mr. Greenbaum. You have a new dress with deep pockets that you love to keep your hands in as you stroll the playground with your best friend. To your horror, the new boy, Smitty, has been making goo-goo eyes at you. You begin to hear rumors on the grapevine about his passion for you. To you, the concept of kissing any boy is the ultimate gross-out. Your sister in the seventh grade says you should try it before you knock it (she's been practicing with Smitty's brother).

DECAF D.U.I. You are a grader driver on a super-highway construction crew and a staunch decaf man. At the morning coffee break you consume three cups of black coffee without realizing it was from the wrong pot. You are ultra-sensitive to caffeine, and your behavior is outrageous whenever you have even one swallow of the stuff. Describe your next grader shift.

HORSE SENSE You see a flier pinned to a bulletin board in a café: *The Horse That Thinks Its Human.* You want to buy that horse. You call the owner and arrange to visit. Give the horse a special name. Where does the horse live? Describe the color of the coat, mane, and tail. Shortly after you arrive, you have a mishap: Something hits you on the skull, dazing you for a brief interlude. You come to and discover that the bump has awoken your psychic powers. What does "The Horse That Thinks Its Human" communicate to you? Do you still want to buy horsy after this surreal conversation?

SO GOOD IT GETS AN OSCAR Your onscreen name is Walter Harrumph-Matthau, and you are starring in a movie called *HULLABALOO!* You're a grumpy old geezer who wants nothing more than to retire and be left alone. Your pathetic long lost nephew, Sherman, shows up on the set lugging his two-year-old kid. Shermy's got a dachshund-with-an-attitude in tow, just to sweeten the deal. Dear Nephew wants to dump them both with you while he chases his wife, who left him because he shrunk her first dachshund. Sound kinda familiar? You've seen the movies, now take liberties with Hollywood's tall tales. Keep in mind that the toddler and the dachshund narrate the action using voice-overs from cartoon characters. (See Footnote #3, page 217, for notes on character copyright.)

MOTHER POWER Railee was raised by her flamboyant and glamorous mother, Giselle, to be fashion-conscious and socially hip. When Railee is twenty-six she has her first child. Somehow, Railee has it encoded in her genes that to be a truly good mother you must be—what?!—frumpy, wholesome, and as steady as the Rock of Gibraltar. She tries to live this ideal while struggling against everything Giselle taught her. Portray Railee's state of mind, her maternal behavior, and her choice of what to wear.

TWIN PARADIGMS One morning, you're lying in bed half awake when a prototype of your body rises from you, strolls into the bathroom and commences to take a shower. After some confusion, you realize that your embodied self is walking around getting ready for the day while you're left to operate with nothing but a ghostly shroud. Your real body doesn't appear to see or hear you, no matter what you try. You can see your body having misunderstandings with other people, but you're helpless to intervene. If only you could get through to yourself, what advice would you give? At other moments, you catch your body doing smart things you never thought of.

PAJAMA PARTY You arrive at work late and sit down in your cubicle. Suddenly, you realize you're still wearing your pajamas. In a panic, you sneak to your boss's office to beg for permission to go home and change. When you gain entry to the inner sanctum, you discover that your boss is wearing *his* pj's. You're too polite to point this out; neither can you bring yourself to ask for permission to go home. Describe your day.

DICK TRACESKI You're a massive skyscraper in New York City. Like the human brain, your mental faculties are located in the penthouse suite. Your heart rides the elevator, you have a million eyes, and your awareness extends beyond your own structure. One fine day your innards alert you to a crime taking place on Level 53. It's an inside job. The criminals make their getaway unseen by the human eye—it's up to you to find a way to have them apprehended. You can see the action unfolding below you in the city streets. Can you save the day?

THE WORLD'S YOUR OYSTER You're a famous author engaged in a national book signing tour. Praise comes in from everywhere. Indulge boastfully in the attention and let it go to your head. Disgust those around you with the true extent of your vanity. Describe a scene with one of your adoring fans.

SELLING PRESTIGE Your name is Leonard Vesl, you're twenty-two years old, and you work as the receptionist in a swanky yacht brokerage. (A yacht broker is like a real estate agent—except transactions are made with yachts instead of houses or land.) Set the scene in your office. Give the brokerage a name and some partners to run it. People the scene with upper crust buyers and sellers. Relate anecdotes illustrating how people react to you in the role of male receptionist. You are always professional on the job. Use your journal to vent and wind down from all the stress. How do the clients make you feel? What do you think of their leisure and wealth?

A THOUSAND & ONE SWORDS You're a proud Arabian swordsman named Ghafir. You are part of an ancient tribe which has eluded modern research—and your tribe plans to keep it that way. The swordsmen use a secret cave as their headquarters, but they live with the main tribe on an everyday basis. Describe your weapon, your clothing, and how you look when mounted on your horse. How do you feel about your tribe? What advice do you give to initiates? What is the role of women and children in your tribe? What do you eat when you're out on a foray party? Who are your enemies? For what reason(s) will you kill another man?

CLOSE ENCOUNTER OF THE FOOD KIND Aliens from the Planet Belliache abduct you, implanting a microchip that allows you to eat as much as you want—without feeling full or putting on weight. A gourmet restaurant three blocks from your house, Café Toulouse, is your favorite place to eat. Discuss what you like to order and where you prefer to sit. What tricks will you stoop to in order to eat there as often as you can without embarrassing yourself? You become aware of other patrons doing 24-7 at Café Toulouse, and you realize the aliens from Belliache must be working the neighborhood. Is anyone motivated to stage a rebellion against this bizarre stomach takeover? Will hot fudge sundae rule the world?

HIPPY-HIPPY-SHAKE-SHAKE In the placid village of Bergsdale, Edward Dullboy is Finance Manager at Town Hall. Edward is conservative, has a strongly developed work ethic and carefully avoids anyone who rocks the boat. The mayor of Bergsdale knows that Dullboy is overworked, and he passes a motion to increase the budget for Edward's department. With these extra funds Town Hall employs a new financial whiz, a young man named Andromeda Smith. As the name implies, Andromeda is unconventional, flexible in his approach to the 8-hour workday and rocks the boat as a matter of principle.

PORTRAIT OF MILADY Mrs. Smoopah is hideously rich and incurably vain, even at the venerable age of eighty-one. You are The Artist Known As Fontainebleau; you take your work very seriously. Mrs. Smoopah commissions you to paint a lavish portrait, planning to bequeath it to her grandchildren when she dies. Mrs. S. wants her Pekingese, Whuf, to appear in the portrait, perched proudly on her lap with a silk ribbon around its "precious" neck—tied before each sitting by yours truly at the old gal's behest. Mrs. Smoopah is difficult enough but Whuf is positively insufferable.

AHEM, MAESTRO Your name's Silas T. Ragsdale, and you have a lucrative studio recording career as a "Body Acoustics" expert. You're highly sought after for your professional sighs, screams, groans, burps, farts, coughs, animal sounds, throat-clearings, sneezes, whistles and yawns. Like a movie star that insists on doing his own stunts, all of your body sounds are pure and authentic. There are no limits to your blazing career. Rock stars book you for background vocals on their albums. Stephen Spielberg has your cell phone number. Kids with Burp-n-Pee dolls beg for your autograph. Your only headache is your agent, B. J. Eckert, that %#$& moralistic prude.

BATTLE OF THE BUDGET Heather and Zak Blowoff are a married couple saving for the first real vacation they've had for almost four years. Heather loves to spend money on her hobbies and believes in getting the most out of every day. Zak is cautious and believes in planning for the future. He designs a strict savings plan, expecting his wife to cooperate. Heather is trying to lose 15 pounds so she can wear revealing sarongs and swimwear during the vacation. Zak studies maps, foreign language books, and travel magazines. He insists *planning* is the best way to make the most of their three-week trip to the Caribbean. Heather prefers to be spontaneous. What happens when it all blows up?

SNIDE AND PREJUDICE You are a male Home Economics teacher; a brand new teacher in an urban school with a tough reputation. Choose a simple recipe, such as scrambled eggs, to demonstrate to your first class. Guide your students through the preparation step by step. These kids are mega cool, and they refuse to be impressed by your culinary skills or be caught laughing at your well-timed jokes. You decide to be as goofy and outrageous as you can be. You'll try anything to get a genuine response.

POOBAH, WARRIOR WOMAN Debbie Delaney has big blue eyes, bouncy blond curls, and a sweet nature. She is the new foreman on the Cruikshank & Hannigan "Super Condo" construction site. The men on this site are not accustomed to being supervised by a girl. They make jokes at Debbie's expense and do plenty of spittin' and cursin'. Uh-oh . . . little do the guys realize what they're in for when Foreman Debbie unleashes her true identity.

SCI-FI GENIUS You are a science fiction writer, and your cranky editor has given you an assignment—to write the next bestseller. You must create a fictional, self-contained world; either in the distant past, the "futuristic" future, or maybe in a parallel dimension. Your world will have its own history and culture totally unrelated to Earth as we know it. In the book, you are the "only living expert," so no one can question your facts or criticize your perceptions—except your crabby editor.

DR. SPOCK IN A DRESS Your name is Paula Mascareña; you teach an evening class to expectant parents. This is not a breathing class for managing labor and childbirth—it's a class on how to raise children. You consider yourself the ultimate authority on the subject, even when it puts noses out of joint. Be as personal, as subjective, and as opinionated on the topic of child-rearing as you need to be. Shock them!

LOWER THAN A SNAKE'S BELLY Jackie Decimal is the head librarian in the small town of Babylon, Arizona, and she is legendary for low self-esteem. Her friends have to listen to her deplore herself ad nauseam. They're so tired of it, they no longer respond like empaths or co-dependants. Instead, they agree with her self-assessments, and they even remind her if she happens to miss any details. Jackie elevates self-criticism to an art form; her angst is of Shakespearean proportions. Unsuspecting strangers find it an ordeal to check out a book from the Babylon library—the tiniest incident can trigger one of Jackie's laments.

BLEEDING HEART Gary Peachy is known as a Chronically Nice Guy. He cheerfully does favors (even behind-the-scenes, unasked-for favors) for everybody he knows, never expecting anything in return. He dispenses compliments and rousing, morale-boosting speeches even under the grimmest circum-stances. He's renowned for his compassionate nature. No one has ever seen Gary Peachy having an angry, sad, or depressed moment. Enter Grimbaldi, the most obnoxious, aggravating, provoking creature ever to crawl out of the old primal soup. Grimbaldi is your creature of choice—human, monster, cock-roach, eel—the species is up to you. Your mission is to provide Gary Peachy with the most challenging day of his life. Will his generosity and compassion survive the grueling spiritual test? Can Grimbaldi withstand 1,000 megawatts of Peachy-power?

DEAR MURPHY You're a fifty-six-year-old widow named Olive Rinehart. Your husband died just before your fifty-third birthday. You were lonely for the first two years, but then you began to date. You love to dance, and at a dinner dance you waltz into a man named Murphy Lowell. You've been dating Murphy for almost nine months now, but his pets are driving you bananas. It's time to write Murph a "Dear John" letter . . . and please be blunt, for the sake of his future girlfriends.

THEM PICNIC BLUES The Dawsons are having their first full family reunion in almost twenty-five years. The reunion is planned for a pine-filled national park on the Oregon coastline. It's summertime, and the first day of the reunion centers around a family picnic. The picnic has been brainstormed and fussed over for many months, so anticipation is rife. Unfortunately, no one in the family gave a thought to consulting the stars—except for the tragically misunderstood horoscope nut, Cousin Cairo. Cousin Cairo tries to warn the family that the day of the picnic will fall at the crux of a Grand Cross Alignment, but alas, no one will listen. (If you'd like a thumbnail sketch of a Grand Cross Alignment to help with your picnic scenario, turn to the profile on page 206.)

ABRACADABRA You are a wizard known to your patrons as Mordikin and your specialty is the weather. Upon request, you produce spells and cloud potions which, when activated, will unleash the desired weather or season of the year. Your spells are popular among clients wishing to influence politics, love affairs, family gatherings, weddings, and so on.

GALLERY ADMISSION You are wandering idly in an art gallery one rainy afternoon. With a jolt of adrenalin, you see a painting that stops you in your tracks. It looks familiar and inviting—as if it has been waiting especially for you. Give the painting a name and describe its scene. Mention how you feel when you look at the painting. You step inside the painting and discover that you can walk around in it. You can even go beyond the parameters that people perceive when they look at the painting as it hangs on the wall. Describe the adventure you have once you're inside the painting. You meet someone you feel magnetized to or obligated to be with. Will you stay? Or does this significant person step out of the painting with you? Either way, how do explain your new life to your family and friends? What about legal ramifications with the gallery?

SHOOTING STAR The year is 1955. Bagley's Comet swings by Planet Earth to say a quick hello on its way to the Vakuna Regis galaxy in Outer Mihnojia. Bagley is visible to the naked eye for two weeks and people are excited. Everybody's throwing comet parties or naming newborn sons after the comet. Meanwhile, it is no party for you: Bagley has over-stimulated your metabolism, and you are unable to sleep for the entire period of heavenly transit. This is no ordinary bout of insomnia, so you don't even bother to go to bed. You are not at all exhausted—in fact, you have plenty of restless energy. While everyone else is asleep, what on Earth will you do to entertain yourself and stay sane for two whole weeks?

RADICAL ROLE REVERSAL You're a six-year-old boy by the name of Dolphin; you have a sassy eight-year-old sister, Mantra. Your mother, Zen Sun-Moon, is a liberal thinker and an outspoken advocate for sexual equality. She refuses to let you play with toy sub-machine guns or plastic soldiers. Instead, she insists that you be given a chance to role-play the nurturing qualities of parenthood the way little girls do when they play with dolls. Your mother encourages you to express your feelings and learn "emotional networking." Mantra's a tomboy—but not because Zen Sun-Moon teaches her to role-play typical male pursuits. Somehow, it doesn't seem fair.

ESCAPISM You are Harry Houdini reincarnated. You have incredible mind control over your bodily functions and can escape from the most impossible predicaments imaginable. But, there's a hitch. You're not a showman like ol' Harry. You are more likely to do what someone else tells you to do than to have a plan or a goal of your own. Relate the tale of your misadventures and the attempts by others to exploit you. Describe exactly how you feel when you are performing one of your amazing feats. Include bodily sensations, voices in your head, the sounds that you make. Focus is your true escapism.

THE RIGHT PERSON FOR THE JOB You were born with absolutely no imagination, you're color blind, and you've never learned to tell the time. Your boss has lumped you with the job of ghostwriting an article which was commissioned by a high-profile magazine. You can't help but make a botch of it. Your boss submits the article in her name without checking a thing. Likewise, the magazine runs the article without checking facts. Meanwhile, your boss can't wait to lap up the credit for writing the article. Her photo will even be on the cover.

COLD OATMEAL & BURNT TOAST Your name is Ruby and you've waitressed in the same joint for twenty-five years. For the past two weeks you've been habitually late for work. Describe why you are late and how you feel when you get to work. How does your boss react? What do your regulars say? Write one scene where you give them lip and one scene where you really surprise them.

WAITER, THERE'S A GREMLIN IN MY SOUP There's an odd noise in your house and you can't get to the bottom of it. At first, you think it's a mouse. You take the usual steps to rid yourself of the pest but the noise persists. Gradually, you get a feeling that this well-concealed creature is playing with your sanity. It uses intelligence and cunning beyond the capabilities of a mere mouse. You are pitting your wits against a diabolical genius! There can be only one winner . . .

SWITCHING CAREERS Minette Rotary is a switchboard operator, the old-fashioned kind who has to plug and unplug each caller with a jack. The switchboard room is the hub of communications for a grand hotel, so Minette's job is busy, busy, busy. The lines are never quiet, and she does a 10-hour shift, six days a week. Minette yearns to be a writer, but her job wears her to a frazzle and she has nothing left to give. She needs a little miracle to bring her dream to life.

SHE'S MINE You have been married for seven years to a very attractive woman. You are possessive of your wife and suspicious of every man who comes within her orbit. You are even jealous of her friendships and the closeness she shares with her family. Describe what she looks like and portray her emotional nature. How does she handle your possessiveness? Do others notice your intensity? Do you believe you should make any efforts to change? If not, describe how others are really at fault and why your smother tactics are necessary.

THE STINK OF POLITICS You are a garbage man named Steinbeck Jones. It is 1959; no one has yet dreamed up fancy titles such as "Waste Disposal Attendant" or "Sanitation Professional" to label your job. There is no technology for lifting devices on the trucks. You hump tin garbage cans in alleys and behind office buildings. You grew up hungry and poor. Your mother named you for the writer, John Steinbeck, and people are always asking why. You've had the same garbage run for years but you've never complained. Suddenly, the department is crawling with politics and the new kid, George, is coveting your run. George happens to be the boss's son . . . you smell trouble ahead.

SPEAK TO ME Camille and Walter Pik are a young married couple with vastly different styles of communication. Camille has always been a talker. She loves high drama, juicy gossip, and expressing herself through extravagant body language. Walter is a serious person who weighs every angle before he speaks. He doesn't even bother to speak unless he deems it "worthwhile." Conversation must be factual to engage his interest. Naturally, he rarely mentions how he feels. Your job is to manufacture a situation which renders Camille speechless while causing Walter to open up and jabber. To build suspense before this amazing turning point, paint a scene or two depicting their typical communication styles.

SIT UP & BEG You are a German shepherd called Ghengis of royal lineage. Your well-meaning but misguided human, Randy, takes you to Polite Pooch Obedience School, and there you are forced to mix company with snotty pampered poodles and other midgets. Your instructor, Ms. Smithers—a smarmy, safari-suited woman—nurses a slyly concealed megalomania complex. She addresses you as "Pookums" and invites you to go for "walkies," but your sixth sense picks up her underlying menace. Poor Randy is besotted with the evil Ms. Smithers and cannot understand where your manners have gone. It's up to you to save Randy—and yourself—from certain doom.

BUTCHER OF THE LANGUAGE Your name is Swanson, and you're a waiter at the Pickled Possum Bar & Grill. You are also a "genius" writing a "bestseller" and expect to be discovered any day now. But the sad truth is, your writing is simply abominable—an embarrassment to the naked eye—but you remain blissfully unaware of this fact. Journal a typical day: Portray your hectic routine juggling two demanding careers. Then work on the outline or compose a page or two from your brainchild—the amazing "page turner" you *know* will be a hit. Have a little soirée with your friends to discuss art, life, and patrons who know how to tip.

SLEIGHT OF HAND Your name is Yolanda Leadbelly, and you're a handwriting analyst for a large company. You have your own office up in the personnel division. The company is pioneering the use of your skills for the hiring and firing of employees and management. So far, they have kept you busy analyzing handwriting samples from the current employee pool. Then, one day, a secret report comes across your desk: Disturbing trends are indicated in the crazy loops and heavy pressure used by the writer. You find out this report was written by Vidor DeBella, Mr. Executive Director himself. What is your next move?

CHEZ PRIDE You are an industrial spy for a ritzy fashion house in gay Paris. There is a big show coming up—a highly prestigious annual event—and competition is fierce. The world-famous designer you spy for prides herself on being a "trendsetter." But you have the inside dope and you know she's not above stealing ideas from other designers. It is a ruthless game and you're the meat in the sandwich. You've found the craftiest place to gather info is to scrutinize the struggling designers who have not yet hit the big time. In your secret travels, you discover a fashion underground—a dimension of rare purity where petty politics and egomania shrivel to nothing. Your patient skullduggery puts you in possession of revolutionary designs. What now?

SCHMUCKDOM NEVER PAYS You are an old woman making a last stand against slimy, sleazy, no-good developers. They want you to leave the home you have inhabited for fifty-seven years so they can bulldoze it and build another shopping mall. They send in their heaviest dude, Mr. Schmuck, to persuade you to leave—but ol' Schmuck wasn't expecting your Chihuahau, Caesar, to be a force to reckon with.

TONSIL TICKLER You're in pain with an abscess in your tooth, but your regular dentist is in Venezuela on vacation. A friend recommends an alternative, and it takes only a day to get an appointment with Dr. Gomer Goldbear. Dr. Goldbear's receptionist, Mitzi, is the strangest gal you've ever met. Sitting in the waiting room is a weird, unsettling experience . . . but it gets weirder. When at last Mitzi ushers you into Goldbear's surgery, you feel as if you bought a ticket to a B-grade show. Dr. Goldbear is a bizarre prankster with a penchant for fake noses. Describe being in the dentist's chair. How do you feel as he works inside your mouth? Talk to your friend on the cell phone after your appointment. Numb mouth or not, be sure to let him know what you think of his precious referral.

THE WORLD IS YOUNG You're three years old and your parents have enrolled you in the local day care center. What is the name of the center? Describe the director of the center and his/her aides. Do you have one favorite teacher? Is there one you hate? Do you rebel or act naughty? Describe some of the playtime activities you participate in—both planned and spontaneous. How do you feel about nap time? Story time? You have a crush on a member of the opposite sex. You also have a three-year-old archenemy. Describe how you interact with these two. Are you glad to go home at the end of the day?

STARBURST You're the highest paid P.A. (Personal Assistant) in Hollywood, and your employer is the most gorgeous woman in Tinsel Town. Flawless skin, cellulite-free thighs, wasp-thin waist, awesome "big hair"—and, yes, world-famous sexy cleavage. She's the nearest thing to a goddess men have ever seen. Unfortunately, her favorite snack is prunes and she binges on them from morn 'til night. She has the worst smelling gas you've ever been trapped with in a sealed limousine. It is your vocation to shelter this dainty goddess from all shock and disappointment. Describe a typical Tuesday at the gym and the gala event she attends that same evening.

COURTROOM FEVER One ordinary afternoon a police officer knocks on the door, reads you your rights, and hauls you off to court. The charge? "Wasting your life." The judge reads you an exhaustive list of what "really matters" in life. The grand irony is this: He has it exactly backwards. You are found guilty of frivolous misuse of time and energy and sentenced to seven years in the clink. From your jail cell, write an appeal for release. Outline what's *really* meaningful in your life and how you promise to use your time if the judge will let you go free. What effect does this rousing document have on your cellmate? Describe what happens when word gets around the prison cellblock. Who comes to see you on visiting day? Some of your visitors want to help you with your appeal, and some don't. . . . But the ones who *don't* want to help work for your freedom are not who you thought they'd be.

GRAND CROSS ALIGNMENT

*Profile Provided by Daniel Carmona**

For optional use with "Them Picnic Blues," page 198. Can also be added to any Fertile Material exercise as a twist.

In a Grand Cross Alignment, Mercury is in retrograde opposed by Uranus; Mars is opposite the Moon.

(Stick with us: It will all make sense in a moment!)

Mercury influences communications. Mercury retrograde is a time to analyze and contemplate rather than a time for action. Uranus is volatile, unpredictable, intuitive. Whenever Uranus influences Mercury then communications will be excited, swift, electric.

Mars is the planet of centrifugal force: a situation of putting out energy and making things happen. With Mars, people express their feelings rather than hold them back.

The Moon is feelings. The Moon is having our needs met. It influences families, eating, and reunions. When you throw in the Moon with the electric communications of Mercury opposed by Uranus, feelings come to the fore. Misunderstandings are then electrically charged and can operate with a domino effect—one misunderstanding triggering another.

*This profile is hypothetical and not intended for any purpose but to dabble in generalities and have some fun.

Qualities of the Planets

MARS

Courageous
Energetic
Angry
Bold
Warlike
Forward
Assertive

MERCURY

Thoughts
Communication
Miscommunication-Rx
Rethinking
Perception
Misperception-Rx
Deep Understanding
Misunderstanding-Rx

URANUS

Unexpected
Unpredictable
Revolutionary
Knowing
Upsetting
Electrical
Insightful
Radical
Intuitive

THE MOON

Feelings
Needs
Family of origin
New beginnings
Mother
Nurturing
Home
Food

Rx = Retrograde

FERTILE MATERIAL
SKELETONS

ABSENTMINDED PROFESSOR Your husband's been neglecting his hairstyle; now he looks like Albert Einstein on a bad hair day.

SIT ON IT You are an armchair in the home of a famous movie director or politician—privy to the secrets of many important people.

PURITY OF THE SPIRIT You live kitty-corner from a chocolate shop; everyday you have to walk past it to get to the post office.

ROACH LOVER You are a cockroach sympathizer giving a speech at a rally for animal rights.

GURU GROOVE You are the beaked head at the top of a totem pole dispensing wisdom to pilgrims who come from afar seeking answers to the mysteries of life.

OBSESSED You are in the fifth grade and shoot marbles religiously—at recess, at lunchtime, and after school.

ACROPOLIS During a layover on a Mediterranean cruise, you propose to your lover in the heady atmosphere of the Parthenon; the famous temple on the hill above Athens.

MODERNISM IN THE RAW You're a famous but arrogant abstract painter forced to defend your work in public.

NEEDLE FREAK You convince a highly conventional member of your family to try acupuncture.

SURVIVAL OF THE WHITEST You're the albino runt in a litter of Doberman pups.

PROUD AND FREE You are the old, royalist flag for a nation in the throes of independence.

FALLEN STAR You are part of a top-notch writing team for a once-popular sitcom now bombing nightly on the air. The producer is acting like a bat out of hell.

DOUBLE VISION You and your 13-month-old twin are being babysat by your grandparents for the weekend.

MATRIARCH CITY You get caught in a time warp and find yourself in a society ruled by women.

WHO, ME? You wake up in a hospital with a temporary case of amnesia.

JULES WAS RIGHT There really is a deep global cavern which opens at the South Pole; you discover it by accident during an out-of-body experience.

IDIOT ON THE BOX You are sitting in your living room watching yourself being interviewed on the evening news.

COCKLE SHELLS & SILVER BELLS You materialize in the bedroom of a child; you're his/her favorite character from a well-loved fairy tale or nursery rhyme.

THE MYSTERIES OF LOVE You've received flowers at work from a secret admirer.

FLYING SLAVE You're a mind-controlled hummingbird used by a secret organization to spy on the enemy.

GOFF You are golfing alone at a Scottish golf course when you run into Sean Connery having a putt.

PUBLIC SPECTACLE You're vain about your looks, and now the doctor says you need glasses.

FREE SPIRIT You are a gypsy wanderer; your home is a hot air balloon.

DRINK ME Someone "slips you a mickey" and you slither into a world of hallucinations.

CINDERELLA HAD IT EASY You are the most unpopular kid in the entire second grade.

BRIDESMAID'S DUTY Your best friend is soon to be married to the same man you recently had a vivid psychic flash about. Should you tell her what you know?

SOCIAL CHILL You're the proud new owner of a 27-foot anaconda; you can't wait for your friends to get acquainted with your pet.

RELUCTANT SURVEILLANCE You are the manager of a department store, and your most trusted employee appears to be shoplifting.

OOPS You've been dating a sexy creature and accidentally find out that he/she wears a wig.

THE POWER . . . OH, AND THE GLORY You are the supreme ruler of a tiny ethnic country where some love you and some hate you.

STAGE FRIGHT Whenever the phone rings you have an uncontrollable urge to let the answering machine answer it. You get stage fright, too, when you have to initiate a call.

ONLY HUMANOID By some miracle you get to spend a day with your ultimate hero, but you uncover truths you wish you didn't have to face.

WASH ME You have organized a charity car wash event, and you seem to be attracting some unusual vehicles.

HONESTY—OR DIPLOMACY? You're the fashion adviser to a pompous personage whose taste is monstrous at best. It's your job to improve your client's public image.

FORTUNE SMILES You're blessed with amazing quirks of good luck and it drives your friends bananas.

BEATLEMANIA You're knocked unconscious and come to on a stage in 1966—in the body of Ringo Starr.

SCARLET WOMAN You're eating dinner in a restaurant with your date (who is wearing white), and you accidentally squeeze the ketchup bottle a little too enthusiastically.

WHAT, NOT AN EGYPTIAN SUN GOD? You sign up for past life regression therapy where you recall that you were once a woolly mammoth in another lifetime.

HERMIT CRAB You're famous, rich, and accomplished but prefer the life of a recluse.

VOICES FROM THE TWILIGHT ZONE You own a 1930's art deco radio; it speaks impulsively without being switched on.

AS JUICY AS THEY COME Your spouse is addicted to fresh mangoes . . . that slurping sound drives you wild and makes you want to kill.

HUMAN LIGHTNING CONDUCTOR It's a sensation in the tabloids: You've been struck by lightning seven times and yet lived to tell the tale.

BOYD'S EYE VIEW You are the star reporter for a popular radio station. You follow your leads via helicopter—with traffic reporting as a bread and butter sideline.

NOWHERE TO HIDE You are painfully timid, but your boss expects you to give the key speech at his 50th wedding anniversary.

A NOBLE BED OF NAILS You are deeply disenchanted with this corrupt society; you take a vow of celibacy for one year as your personal statement of protest.

BAH, HUMBUG The local preschool talks you into dressing up as Santa Claus so the kids can sit on your lap at the Christmas party and give you their wish lists.

FERTILE MATERIAL FOR YOUR SERIOUS MOODS

CLIFFHANGER You're out hiking in the mountains. Some shale slips under your feet, and suddenly you're sliding down a steep embankment. Describe how you feel as you slide. It's a rough landing and you are injured. How do your companions react? Are you calm or upset? Is your speech lucid? You need help right away. How can the nearest Search & Rescue team be notified? When they do arrive, how do you feel about your rescuers? Describe how they bring you to safety. What effect does this mishap have on your life?

GENTLE GUIDE You've been blind since birth, and you have a guide dog named Vinnie. Describe the act of taking a walk with Vinnie along a city street. Go fully into the sensory realms: tell us how it feels, what it sounds like. Describe an encounter with someone who pities you. You also hear a reaction from a child out walking with his mother. What have you learned through living as a blind person that sighted people seem to miss?

COLD BLOODED? You are walking near a river with your family and the family dog. A member of your group disturbs a snake protecting its eggs. Everyone has a different emotional response to what's happening, and the riverbank is in an uproar. Portray the mother snake's behavior. Be specific about each family member's reaction to the snake.

MARK OF SELF-ESTEEM You were born with a large, raspberry-colored birthmark on your face. Mention the specific areas of your face that it covers. How do you feel about your birthmark? Describe a time from childhood when someone singled you out to remark upon it. Describe a time from adulthood when you attempted to conceal your birthmark.

ORDINARY SLICE You have been a homemaker for nineteen years. Your mother brought you up to be compliant, and your husband expects you to keep the same routine day in and day out. Your hobbies are knitting, collecting recipes, and watching travelogues on TV. One day you look in the mirror and realize you're still young. What else do you realize? What actions do you take? How does your husband respond to your feelings and your actions?

FIT TO PRINT You've read an exposé about the ways the nightly news is alleged to be doctored and biased. You get all fired up and feel like going on the talk show circuit to express your opinion. You're an anonymous citizen with no skeletons in the closet and no sexual ostentation to offer. The television studios pass you over in favor of the "real" ratings generators. Just when you're feeling powerless to make a difference, your uncle dies; his will bequeaths you a newspaper syndicate. You now have the means to print whatever you want to say and to influence millions.

TO SEND MILLI A SAMPLE OF YOUR FERTILE MATERIAL

This exchange is not about writing advice, career boosters, or finding a publishing contract. It's about having your own friendly, non-critical audience.

Please keep to the spirit of this enterprise and submit only Fertile Material stories. Milli will delete all screenplays, novels, and other unsolicited manuscripts not based on the Fertile Material exercises.

Do not submit more than 5 typewritten pages, but single-spaced is fine. Don't worry about using the proper manuscript formatting—this is purely for the pleasure of having someone read and acknowledge your work. Milli encourages you to submit your story "raw" (i.e., with little or no editing). Email your story or vignette to:

fertilematerial@fearofwriting.com

In your cover email, please note the reason for submitting your sample.* Allow 2-3 weeks for Milli's response.

*Readers submitting material for the sequel(s) should check the website for submission guidelines: www.fearofwriting.com.

ABOUT THE AUTHOR

Venus Masci © 2000

MILLI THORNTON was born in Wallace, Idaho in 1960 and has suffered from fear of writing for most of her life. She migrated to Australia with her family at age twelve, where she discovered that "blue" means redhead and "billy" is a tin you brew bush tea in. She sampled a variety of home bases, including Coffs Harbour, Sydney, Darwin, Melbourne, Airlie Beach on the Barrier Reef, and the Blue Mountains. After 25 years in her beloved Australia, Milli returned to the United States to reunite with her scattered family. She lived for five years in the mountains of New Mexico with her husband and two cats, where she ate chimichangas and sopapillas instead of prawns, snags, and pavlova. She went bush (returned Down Under) in 2003, where she's savoring Vegemite, boxing with the 'roos, and giving that famous Aussie salute—swatting bush flies!

Visit the photo gallery at Milli's website to see her Aussie writing and bushwalking adventures. The gallery and journal records her two-week stint working on the sequel at Varuna Writers' Retreat in the gorgeous Blue Mountains of New South Wales. Admission to the gallery is free: www.fearofwriting.com.

GRAMMAR & PUNCTUATION: A HAPPY FOOTNOTE
The spirit of the Fertile Material can be killed with the use of dictionaries or grammar rulebooks. But for those times when it truly matters (i.e., when submitting manuscripts to writing contests and publishers) Milli recommends *What's the Rule?** by Kathy Sole, at www.whatstherule.com.

FOOTNOTE 2: MUSIC FOR CREATIVITY
As she wrote the section "Chanting the Douhm," Milli was feeling creatively inspired by the CD called *Sunrise** by Phil Jones. The album features Australian didgeridoo, Scottish bagpipe, Irish tin whistle, Tibetan gong, the lap drum, and the Native American flute. http://philjonesmusic.com.

FOOTNOTE 3: CHARACTER COPYRIGHT
For exercises such as "Duello" (p. 107), and in reference to movie or TV characters: If you're worried about copyright, it's wiser not to use the original character names or movie title; unless in parody. If you decide to try to publish a story using characters from another media, check Myth 6 of the *10 Big Myths About Copyright Explained** Web feature: www.templetons.com/brad/copymyths.html. Still unsure? Seek legal advice. But don't contact the author of *10 Myths*, Brad Templeton (his own footnote is emphatic that he does not give legal advice).

FOOTNOTE 4: AUTHOR'S PERMISSION TO USE THE FERTILE MATERIAL EXERCISES Milli Thornton gives her consent to readers of *Fear of Writing* to use the Fertile Material exercises to write their own vignettes and stories. Milli likewise gives permission to the users of the Fertile Material to publish their own Fertile Material creations—as long as due credit is given for the source of the inspiration.

---

*The author is under no financial inducement to recommend this tool.

INDEX OF THE FERTILE MATERIAL

Made in the USA